Presented to

_____

By

_____

On the Occasion of

_____

Date

Grab a Broom, Lord...
There's Dust Everywhere!

The Imperfect Woman's Guide to God's Grace

Karon Phillips Goodman

BARBOUR
PUBLISHING

ISBN 978-1-58660-918-4

Published by Barbour Publishing, Inc., P.O. Box 719, Uhrichs-
ville, Ohio 44683, www.barbourbooks.com

*Our mission is to publish and distribute inspirational products offer-
ing exceptional value and biblical encouragement to the masses.*

Member of the
Evangelical Christian
Publishers Association

Printed in the United States of America.

Dedication

*To my son, who never
fails to see past my dust.*

Contents

Introduction

Thanks be to God for His indescribable gift!

2 Corinthians 9:15 NKJV

Oh, to be perfect! Wouldn't that be wonderful? Wouldn't it be great to always do the right things and say the right things and make the right choices and never need any help? Wouldn't it be great if your past was missing even the tiniest indiscretion and your future was immune to even the slightest mistake? It probably *would* be great—too bad it's also impossible. That kind of perfection never has happened, never will.

But like a settler panning for gold, we keep hoping for it anyway. How often have you cried over your failures and mistakes that you can't change? How many times have you wished that you could be free of all your flaws and insecurities, your painful past and recurring trespasses? How many times have you looked at yourself in the mirror and seen a wicked, weak, and worthless face staring back at you? Well, you'll have to get in line. I'm at the very front.

What makes it so hard for us to accept and deal with our imperfections, setbacks, and mistakes? And why do we so often refuse the one thing that could comfort us? Every time we tend the wounds of our lives alone and isolate ourselves from the Lord instead of turning to Him for help, He cries with us and wonders why we can't understand and accept the gift only He can give.

The Lord stands ready to help us with our imperfections because He understands them so well. He *created* us imperfect. (He got a little carried away with some of us, but I'll trust that He has a plan. . . .) He knows that we'll fail Him and ourselves from time to time. But He's prepared. Our imperfections don't have to stop us from enjoying the amazing life He's given us and from doing what we were born to do. He's got them covered.

There is much work for all of us to do, and we can begin when we believe and accept that God can use us *no matter what.* Because our human nature tends to think in terms of what we earn and deserve, we sometimes just run from God when we've failed, feeling unworthy and too far from His grasp. But He's still there, saying, "Whoa, hold on a minute, let's talk about it. . . ." He provides the only way that we can deal with our imperfections: His indescribable *grace*. Perhaps it would be wonderful to be perfect, to never fail again, to never need God's grace. Then again, perhaps not. . .

In these pages, we'll look at how we can overcome this need for perfection, deal with the past, live the present, and embrace the future. We can handle our unending mortal imperfection with attention to our *attitude, application,* and *appreciation* of God's immortal grace. Nothing else will ever work.

What a blessed relief it is to just *accept* that we can't be perfect or do everything perfectly— and that God never meant for us to! He has a way around our human weaknesses, a way to clean up the messes we make and find some use in us anyway.

There is always life after lapses, no matter how much they hurt. Do you want the Lord to sweep up your imperfections and help you get your life on track? Do you want to be more *useful* than perfect? Please join me here and we'll do it together.

The grace of our Lord was poured out
on me abundantly,
along with the faith and love that are
in Christ Jesus.

1 TIMOTHY 1:14 NIV

Sure, God could have made us independent and stoic, but instead He made us imperfect and needy. With the entire universe at His disposal, He made us a frame of dust. Yet this feeble frame can house His very soul and Spirit. That makes us better than perfect. That makes us loved.

Part 1

"Why'd You Give Me This Rickety Ole Frame in the First Place?"

The *Attitude* of God's Grace

For He knows our frame;
He remembers that we are dust.

PSALM 103:14 NKJV

"Pardon the interruption, Lord, but I have a question. Being omnipotent and all powerful as

13

You are, able to make impenetrable mountains and raging seas, can You please explain why You made *me* so weak and faulty? I try so hard to be good, and yet I make so many mistakes and fail for all the world to see. And the inside is even a bigger mess than the outside. I am as weak as dust scattered in the wind, as needy as a newborn. Any chance for a recall?"

"You want to question My design?"

"Uh, that's not what I meant. . . ."

"You are *exactly* the way I made you to be. The earth and the sea have no need for Me. I breathed them strong and self-sufficient. Yes, you are fragile in comparison, but you have something they don't. You have a need for My soul. It's a need that you fight now and then; yet it is one that you cannot avoid. Yes, you are as weak as dust, but I made you that way so that you would need *Me*. My soul lives because of your need."

"But look at this dust all around me. I can't clean it up. . . ."

"I know. Do I look worried? I have the only broom you'll ever need."

"Are You sure? I'm a *big* mess."

"I have a big broom."

* * * * *

Chapter 1

He's Not Surprised!

"For I am the LORD,
I do not change."

MALACHI 3:6 NKJV

Well, that was quite a revelation! What enlightenment! For years, I've fought my imperfections and tried to correct them and eliminate them all by myself. And yet, it can't be done. No matter how hard I try, I still fail. I still make mistakes, still hurt those I love, still misunderstand and suffer my own hurts, still spill dust *everywhere* while I clumsily plod along, day by day, with this helpless housing of my soul.

And what is the Lord doing while I flail about uselessly, like a fish trying to fly? He's standing there with a broom and a gift.

I must appear so ungrateful, but my reasoning has been skewed for so long: "I need to be stronger, without so many problems and shortcomings, better at everything I'm trying to do, quicker to realize my errors. . . ." These have been my thoughts day and night as I've cursed my failures and stood ready to listen to God's disappointment as well as my own. You'd think He would share my concerns. . . .

And yet, no. He seems rather unsurprised and unperplexed by my inabilities and short-comings, while they frustrate and depress me to no end! Never very efficient at anything else, I've always been the first to recognize my horrible deeds. Then as if I could hide them from God, I'd sneak around and try to improve myself without bothering Him.

I'd imagine wrapping my tiniest steps toward perfection in a box pretty enough to present to the Lord and watch Him smile in approval. I can't tell you how many times I played that little game. A day when I could show myself perfect to Him, by the way, hasn't happened *yet*.

And it gets worse. Instead of climbing some mountain of perfection in my mind, I keep failing. Every day, I fail at something (because there is always so much to do and I'm a slow learner); and every day, if I allow it, I become even more insecure, afraid, wondering when God's tolerance of my imperfection will finally come to an end. But that day hasn't happened yet, either. What *is* the Lord's reaction to the messes I make?

He grabs a broom.

Our willingness to seek His grace (and eventually, our dependence on it) is what He craves. It's not perfection from us that He expects, but trust and growth and discipleship—a request for *His unique help*. He wants the best we can do, each new day, with this frame of dust held together by our Maker. That's enough. That's the key—to understand our dependence on Him, not to impress Him with our lack of need. Why would that, of all things, make us more valued or loved?

> *Not that we are sufficient of*
> *ourselves to think of anything*
> *as being from ourselves,*
> *but our sufficiency is from God.*

2 CORINTHIANS 3:5 NKJV

 It's All Part of the Plan

What absurd notions we come up with sometimes though. . . . How could we possibly think that we could put on our best spit and polish and impress the Lord with something we've accomplished on our own? It makes me shake my head to entertain such a thought. No wonder we try to hide our flaws if that's the best kind of reasoning we have!

I've done it, though, and I bet you have, too—tried to "get better" before going to God. *I'll just clean up this one mess and then I won't be so unpresentable,* we think. And God says, "Huh? The sooner she comes to Me, the sooner I can help her."

We have it all backward! *It's not about getting better to go to God; it's about going to God to get better.*

And yet we want to reinvent ourselves *our* way instead, questioning that the Lord knew what He was doing when He brought us here. He must have, though, since "we are God's workmanship, created in Christ Jesus to do good works" (Ephesians 2:10 NIV). That sounds like He had the recipe for our creation pretty well under control, doesn't it?

I know what you're thinking—*but my mess hardly looks like the workmanship of God!* I know that mess. (I've lived that mess!) It looks hopeless to us because we're always looking from the bottom of the pile of dust. God looks past it, around it, and over it, and says, "Come here, stand still a moment, I have a plan. . . ."

The plan was in place before you were. If He had wanted you to live your life self-sufficient and alone, He would have made you so. You'd be a mountain or a wave or a star. He would have changed you when He created you.

Instead of free will, you would have an inner rudder that stole from you the thrill of discovering His grace, personal and unique to meet your needs.

Instead of an innate will to grow, you would be content to live a life incomplete and shallow, never knowing the blessings of a grace-filled God.

Instead of a trust in Him, you would live with the unsatisfying emptiness that denies His existence. Instead of a desire for Him, you would feel the pain of a world where He is unknown. Instead of a thirst to understand Him, you would trust your inferior intellect and knowledge.

Instead of a belief in Him, you would live and die alone, untouched by the grace He so freely gives. " 'I am the resurrection and the life. He who believes in Me, though he may die, he shall live. And whoever lives and believes in Me shall never die. Do you believe this?' " (John 11:25–26 NKJV).

We want the absolute acceptance the Lord stands ready to give, and yet our human urge for self-sufficiency surfaces all too often. We believe in God and worship Him from afar, but we still sometimes don't want to *need* Him so much. We're embarrassed by our failures and impatient with ourselves because we can't do everything perfectly and on our own. The pain that our failures bring can make us feel that we're beyond God's grasp and incapable of His holy work. We don't feel comfortable asking for anything.

We know God is good, but we sometimes think He has limits. We believe that we've been blessed an allotted amount and that we should now, at whatever arbitrary age we've chosen, be capable of managing on our own and not make any more mistakes. That's a neat and tidy theory. It's also hogwash, but it's neat and tidy hogwash.

And all the while we try to bathe ourselves in it, the Lord is sitting there wondering why, holding the broom that can clean everything. He isn't surprised or deterred when we're not perfect or when we need His help. We don't have to be, either.

Hear my cry, O God; attend to my prayer.
From the end of the earth I will cry to You,

when my heart is overwhelmed;
lead me to the rock that is higher than I.

PSALM 61:1–2 NKJV

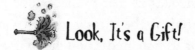

Look, It's a Gift!

I love presents. I love giving presents and getting presents, and I can rarely wait for Christmas or someone's birthday when I think I've found the perfect gift. And if someone gives me something, it doesn't matter what it is. I'm always touched by the expression of kindness, accepting a wonderful present from someone who loves me "just because."

But for some reason, I am often hesitant to accept from the Lord that which I can't earn (which is everything, but let's stay on track here). As if possessed by a work ethic on steroids of guilt, I think that I can only approach God if I've put in my time and justified my existence enough to ask for His help. Do you know that feeling, too?

It's as if we take a little literary license with the Scriptures, when we can plainly see "for all have sinned and fall short of the glory of God,

21

and are justified freely by his grace" (Romans 3:23–24 NIV). What generosity! What acceptance! And yet, those of us who know what He *really* meant sometimes see it this way: "For all have sinned," but that probably doesn't include *me*. I need to be strong enough and smart enough and talented enough—whatever—not to fall short; and because I'm a bit worse than anyone else, I fall too far outside the grace of God to be redeemed. I'll just wait on the outside, looking in, until I'm better.

The lengths we'll go to, to try to take care of the dust ourselves! We can rewrite those words all we want, but it doesn't change them. The Lord didn't say we'd be flawless and never need His grace, but that we all fall short. It is a simple acknowledgment of our failures; and what follows isn't a rebuke or a punishment, but instead a promise: that we'd be justified *freely* by His grace—not at a cost, not when we earned it, not when we deserved it—but immediately, *freely*.

He knew we'd live in this imperfect world with our imperfect selves facing imperfect situations. Look at His preparation and compensation for our weaknesses, great long-range planner that

He is. Look at how He's dressed these faulty frames of ours:

> *For He has clothed me with the garments*
> *of salvation, He has covered me*
> *with the robe of righteousness.*
>
> ISAIAH 61:10 NKJV

That's not a picture of someone perfect and without need, someone who does everything right, always on time and without help. That's a picture of a creation of dust loved by the Creator—not because of her perfection, but in spite of her lack of it, because of her soul and her need. God loves us enough to "cover" and "clothe" us in His very being. You'd think we'd grab at those coverings every second of the day!

But what do we do? We stand here, hanging our heads, licking our wounds, taking our time and energy that should be spent on our work, and instead using it to try to clean up our mess ourselves. It's like trying to swim ashore in a hurricane when there's a perfectly good rescue boat right beside us, full of rescuers whose only purpose is to carry us to safety. And what do we do? We kick harder to try to prove that we don't really need any help after all. Thanks for asking, though.

When we're thinking clearly, we may acknowledge that God's grace is a wonderful gift given to all His children. Then on other days, we believe that it's withheld from us because we're somehow different, just *too* imperfect, a little *too* unworthy. The fact is, none of us is worthy of God's grace; but it makes no difference to the Lord because He pours out the grace by the bucketfuls anyway, not because we're worthy, but because we're *not*.

> *For it is by grace you have been saved,*
> *through faith—*
> *and this not from yourselves,*
> *it is the gift of God.*
>
> EPHESIANS 2:8 NIV

That we don't deserve such generosity makes it even harder for us to understand why the Lord gives it anyway. Still, He *gives* it—there is no way that we can earn His grace or His coverings. It can't be done because the Lord's grace, by definition, is a *gift*, given out of intense love by the God "who has saved us and called us to a holy life—not because of anything we have done but because of his own purpose and grace. This grace was given us in Christ Jesus before the beginning of time" (2 Timothy 1:9 NIV).

Before you were even born, God gave you the gifts to live a life holy, to show your love for Him, and to serve others through the ministry He chose for you. But He didn't give you the gift of perfection, and He never will in this life because you don't need it. Instead, He gives you grace without end.

* * * * *

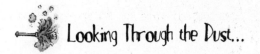 Looking Through the Dust...

- Which of your imperfections or mistakes bothers you the most? How have you been dealing with them?
- What have you tried to accomplish or correct without "bothering" God? How's that going so far?
- In which areas of your life can you look back and see how you tried to do everything alone? Can you see that God was there all along?

25

- Why have you been afraid or reluctant to seek and accept the gift of God's grace?

* * * * *

Lord, in Your grace, *please help me learn about Your most beautiful gift, the gift that I will never deserve and You will never deny. Amen.*

Chapter 2

Why We're This Way

*In him we have redemption through his blood,
the forgiveness of sins, in accordance with the
riches of God's grace that he lavished on us
with all wisdom and understanding.*

EPHESIANS 1:7–8 NIV

I can remember crying every night over my school-work when I was in the first grade. If I reached the end of the page and made a mistake, I wouldn't erase and correct it—I'd start over. No matter how many pages it took or how long I worked, I always had to have a perfect page to turn in.

My parents worried about me and even took me to a doctor who prescribed some kind of foul-tasting medicine. Eventually, I learned to use an eraser and managed to complete first grade without need of a psychiatrist. My parents, and everyone else, still called me a perfectionist. I honestly didn't have a clue why—I thought I was normal.

Was that kind of perfection expected of me? Of course not. Was I expected to know everything and not ever need any help with my work? Again, of course not. But it didn't matter to me, because the expectations of perfection were *mine*.

And I hate to admit this, but my obsession actually got worse before it got better. My need to control and perfect everything that touched me lasted well into adulthood. When I was sure that even my *garbage* had to be put out a certain way, it finally became clear even to me that I needed a better approach to my life. Finding it took years.

I might have thought I had it all together, but all I had was a nervous stomach and an expectation of myself that built a wall so high and thick that God Himself probably had a hard time looking over it.

I could barely tolerate my slightest flaws— how could Almighty God stand to even consider the idea? And yet He would even go farther than that, to not only forgive me and accept me, but to look upon me as new and capable, to allow me to do His work, still, in my imperfect condition. Why? Because it's what He *does*. Thank the Lord!

He grants His grace. Our job is to accept it graciously and get back to work. "Therefore, if anyone is in Christ, he is a new creation; old things have passed away; behold, all things have become new" (2 Corinthians 5:17 NKJV).

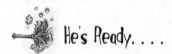

He's Ready. . . .

If the Lord stands willing to grant us grace and strength and guidance to carry on, why are we so determined to argue with Him, to question His goodness and willingness to give?

What *is* it that makes us want to hide the dust and sweep up the mess we make ourselves, to feel as if we're saddled with a thousand impossible tasks that we should miraculously and immediately know how to accomplish? Human frailty? Innate insecurities? Fear? Unreasonable expectations? All of the above?

Probably so, but mostly just a flawed

interpretation. Maybe you can relate. . . .

Sometimes, we probably all sound like this: "The worst part is feeling that I'm the only being in the universe who has made such a mess of her life (yes, others have made messes, too, but I can excuse their dust piles—mine is *really* big and bad). So I look at history, from the world's beginning through yesterday, and decree that everyone else can share in God's riches, but I'm just not included in that lucky group yet. After all, look at me—I've failed at everything. I'm a mess!"

And on and on it goes. Do you know that weight of isolation that pulls you down, that attitude that speaks only of your imperfection and ignores God's perfect ability to deal with it? I thought so.

He knows when we're feeling that way, and yet He's not afraid of what He sees. He's not moved by our doubts. I imagine that He wonders why, when we could seek His grace with one breath, we instead put our efforts through a sausage grinder and come out with a sentence of "no grace for me," no reprieve, no mercy. We're confused, but He's still the same. We resist; He remains.

I'm sure He clearly remembers giving us the mind and the heart to *want* to accept His goodness. But He's familiar with our hesitation and He understands our fear. He waits for us to peek over the dust and breathe to Him a call of, "Lord, please. . ."

> *But you are a shield around me, O LORD;*
> *you bestow glory on me and lift up*
> *my head. To the LORD I cry aloud,*
> *and he answers me from his holy hill.*

PSALM 3:3–4 NIV

 . . .But We Doubt and
Make It So Hard

We struggle, and yet the Lord gives us His amazing grace when we need it, speaking to us through His unmatchable love so that we can overcome our dust and carry on. He knows we're going to falter from time to time—I'm sure He has season tickets to *my* failures—but to God, it's not about the falling. It's about the getting up and trying again, dust and all. It's about the choice to "press on to take hold of that for which Christ Jesus took hold of me" (Philippians 3:12 NIV).

We can only "press on" with the grace of God. Sometimes, though, we stand stopped in our tracks, covered with the dust that we won't allow the Lord to sweep away. Of course, we need to learn from our mistakes and misjudgments and hopefully not repeat them, but we cheat God and ourselves when we let those imperfections block us from His grace and the strength to try again. No matter how many times we fall, God's there. We wonder if He'll really stay for *us*. See if this sounds familiar:

We're so programmed to question His unbelievable generosity that we often find it strangely comforting to exile ourselves from Him since we've failed Him and ourselves so horribly anyway. The result is a standstill, a lock on our reason for being—actually, a veiled question of God's unfailing judgment. He's probably not real pleased when we surround ourselves with walls of guilt that we won't let Him penetrate. But we know the practice well, living in a self-imposed jail that's hard to escape. After all, we've been building it for years.

Instead of going to the right place for help

and destroying that prison, like a fad diet fan, we just try a new solution. We devise a new plan that will help us, this time, we're sure, to be "good enough." But what happens instead? We still fail every minute, not because we don't try, but because we aren't capable of reaching the expectations of perfection we set for ourselves. And we're not happy about, but completely accustomed to, the defeated feeling these attempts bring. Perhaps you know the drill?

Perhaps you know about living in that prison and wishing that you could allow yourself to feel God's grace, but the fear is too great. What if He decides to make an exception out of *you?* What if the rules have changed? What if your pile of dust is just too high? I know the thought—*He hasn't changed His mind since the creation of the world, but maybe for me. . .*

Do you really think God would make a mistake in lavishing you with "the riches of His grace"? If He does so at His will, "with all wisdom and understanding," then it cannot be a mistake. Aren't we blessed that He can be nothing but perfect?

Still, logic doesn't help us obsessive types sometimes. We'd rather just be perfect and not need to ask for help in the first place. We *can't* understand why it couldn't just be that way, and then things would be so much tidier. . . . The Lord's heavy sigh on that one comes in loud and clear!

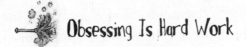

Obsessing Is Hard Work

Turn to me and be gracious to me,
for I am lonely and afflicted.
The troubles of my heart have multiplied;
free me from my anguish.

PSALM 25:16–17 NIV

Trying to be perfect may be useless, but it makes us very good at one thing—construction! This uncomfortable cell that we build for ourselves comes with a couple of strong beliefs that wall us away from God and our work.

First, we can't even comprehend the phrase: "Don't be so hard on yourself." We can't entertain the idea of giving ourselves a break when we fail to reach that unreachable summit or when we make a misstep. We'd flog ourselves if we knew how.

On top of this belief that we should be perfect,

we decide that we should reach this perfection all by ourselves. Completely alone. Without any help from anyone. Especially God. Our prayers are more "please don't look" than "please help me."

It gets better: Perhaps the saddest part in this whole obsession with perfection is that we alone hold this expectation. We've created this unrealistic need for sainthood here on earth, all unnecessarily, all painful, all pointless. We've devised this ever-changing picture of ourselves that rises and falls on any particular day's level of perfection. And we measure regularly. If we're relatively free of sin today, we'll allow ourselves to stand a little taller and even venture a timid smile.

But if we've had even the *slightest* misstep, we're in a hole so deep that we won't even try to see out of it. And when we really mess up—look out! There is absolutely no consoling us because we don't *deserve* any consolation. We've fallen completely off God's radar, and that's where we belong anyway!

And on those rare occasions when we feel that we're not so bad, no matter how "good" we are or how many "good deeds" we do, we're still one foot in the hole, not quite ready to allow ourselves entry or residence into the world of

God's grace. (While hopeless at everything else, we believe we're quite capable of deciding when, if ever, that will be.) We're just never good *enough*.

> *For no other foundation can anyone*
> *lay than that which is laid,*
> *which is Jesus Christ.*
>
> 1 CORINTHIANS 3:11 NKJV

"I'm not there yet," we think to the Lord. "Doesn't matter," He replies, "*I* am."

What Makes Us This Way?

The harsh judgment that we apply to every aspect of our lives can be awfully confining. Worse than the most overactive conscience, it keeps us separated and afraid, wounded and ashamed. But that's not the purpose of knowing right from wrong. Instead our judgment should give way to submission, propel us in only one direction, to the only Being capable of cleaning up the mess.

When my heart was grieved
and my spirit embittered,
I was senseless and ignorant;
I was a brute beast before you.
Yet I am always with you;
you hold me by my right hand.
You guide me with your counsel,
and afterward you will take me into glory.
Whom have I in heaven but you?
And earth has nothing I desire besides you.
My flesh and my heart may fail,
but God is the strength of my heart
and my portion forever.

PSALM 73:21–26 NIV

I know, I know. You want to go there, to the Lord so big and strong; but the practice of years of indoctrination into the "look at all I've done wrong" school of thought keeps getting in the way of that first step.

And like most perfectionists, I imagine that you're quite sure that you *really are* a mess that tests God's patience. Don't worry—I've already stretched Him for you.

I, too, know that feeling of despair, and it's hard to shake. The belief that we're too far from

God's grace is heavy and strong, piled high on the dust that we cannot avoid. To even try to attempt to understand or accept our dust seems tantamount to making excuses—and we perfectionists don't allow that very often!

But the Lord doesn't spend His time placing blame for our weakness. "Deal with it," He says, "this way." He wants us to grow and overcome and continue our journey with Him on the wings of His grace and in the safety of His love.

He makes it look so simple. We complicate it every chance we get—not with our dust, but with our brooms even weaker than our frames. We try to do what we can't. "The man who thinks he knows something does not yet know as he ought to know. But the man who loves God is known by God" (1 Corinthians 8:2–3 NIV).

So while we stand constantly perplexed and annoyed by our failures, God's reaction isn't hopelessness, but love and grace that forgive and teach. "Come to Me and we'll make it better," He says. We wallow in our mess while He stands eager to sweep it away, but we don't know if we should let Him. As stubborn as a season change, we'll gladly take the blame, but "hold the grace, please, we don't deserve it."

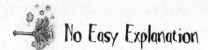

No Easy Explanation

Maybe this seemingly inescapable need for perfection stems from a deep sense of justice or responsibility or honor. Who knows? But you know it when you have it. We may not understand why we feel this way, but you and I can be very different and still both have this same obsession. It usually starts when we're little, and it only grows as we do. With the strength of a crocodile's bite, it holds on tightly and can be just as damaging.

Sometimes we struggle through our teen years or sometimes we glide through them unscathed. Maybe our young adulthood is tumultuous or maybe it's a breeze. Becoming a more mature woman may come with tough challenges or it may be an easy part of life. The funny thing is, *it doesn't seem to matter,* because we can always find some flaw that keeps us outside God's reach. We're never short of imperfections.

Whether our past was littered with painful failures and unfulfilled dreams or just the fairly typical rite of passage, *it doesn't matter.* We beat up on ourselves (quickly before anyone else can, since we do it so much better anyway), and we stand ready to take our punishment, desperate enough to ask for God's grace but afraid to accept it in all its grandeur. How *dare* we infringe on His time when we should have never made this mess in the first place!

> *"Behold, I am the LORD,*
> *the God of all flesh.*
> *Is there anything too hard for Me?"*
>
> JEREMIAH 32:27 NKJV

There is certainly much that appears to be too hard for us—seeing around this gigantic pile of dust we've created, for starters. We made it, so we must dissect it and sift it and analyze it and make hopeless attempts to dissolve it. Because we have to. We'll never settle for not accepting responsibility for our choices, and that's okay; but we tend to stretch the other way with the tenacity of a telemarketer.

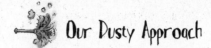

Our Dusty Approach

Time to bring out the clipboard and check the list: How many mistakes have we made this last hour? Only that many? That's not bad, but look at the hour before that. And there's still the page from yesterday. . . . It never ends!

Of course, we should look at ourselves honestly, and we can always find ways to improve and make better choices. But our unhealthy need for and obsession with perfection actually *blocks* us from God's grace instead of leading us to it. The dust pile grows while we refuse to believe that it can disappear.

Accepting our imperfection is the first step in seeking God's grace. Then we must trust Him to accept it as well and to do what only He can. All of this acceptance comes, first, to prepare you with the open heart and receptive spirit into which the Lord can extend His grace—yes, even to messy lives like yours and mine.

We must believe that He sees past our imperfections, or we can't fully receive His grace—because you can't accept that which you

don't believe will be given to you. And He so
wants to give!

> *The LORD is my shepherd; I shall not want.*
> *He makes me to lie down in*
> *green pastures;*
> *He leads me beside the still waters.*
> *He restores my soul.*
>
> PSALM 23:1–3 NKJV

Again, it doesn't matter how horrid we
believe our transgressions to be or how far away
we've wandered, God the Shepherd will find us
and restore us because we're all the same. Your
weight is just as heavy as mine, regardless of
which one of us has made the "bigger" mistake
on some nonexistent scale or which one of us
makes the "bigger" mess each day we try not to.
When the mistakes are ours, they're all tragic and
seemingly impossible to overcome. They are a
constant reminder of our frame so frail and
weak—and how likely it is that it always will be.

Guess what? It's as strong as it needs to be.
It's strong enough to say, "Here I am, Lord." He
takes care of the rest. "For when I am weak, then
I am strong" (2 Corinthians 12:10 NKJV).

42

The Lord's Strength Is Enough

*"I know that You can do everything,
And that no purpose of Yours
can be withheld from You."*

JOB 42:2 NKJV

Taking responsibility for your mistakes doesn't mean that you have to package and display them in the very front of your mind and your heart and take inventory every day. That might work if we were even remotely capable of reconciling our own faults. But if we could do that, we wouldn't need God. And that's not how He designed us.

Responsibility means going to Him with your dust and asking for forgiveness, understanding, and direction. Responsibility is never about living a solitary life, self-sufficient and without need of something bigger than you are.

Are you beginning to see how this works? It's amazing that we fight it for so long. Maybe it's because we don't want to acknowledge our dust—I certainly have a pile or two I'd like to forget. But of course, it's pointless because the dust will collect until we allow God to sweep it away.

He'll leave the pile there until you point to it and say, "Yeah, I did that. Can You help me?" And then, before you can finish your breath, it's gone. Just like that. And His next words are about the future, not the past. "Now, get back to work," He says.

God's grace is given without restraint, a salvation to us who could never earn it. You can't ever work hard enough to deserve it, but you can't go on without it. The Lord provides the only way— call it a cure, a treatment, an escape, a guiding light—anything you want. But know that the Giver who gives this free gift knows exactly how much you need and when you need it. He deals with your dust in the unique way that you need Him to, and it's *always enough*. Ask.

> *"Ask and it will be given to you;*
> *seek and you will find;*
> *knock and the door will be opened to you.*
> *For everyone who asks receives;*
> *he who seeks finds; and to him who knocks,*
> *the door will be opened."*

MATTHEW 7:7–8 NIV

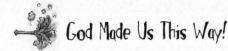

God Made Us This Way!

The Lord is the ultimate CEO. He knows everything without being told. He keeps His eye on the bottom line. He has the entire plan already mapped out. He can delegate without overpowering. There is nothing about us that He doesn't know. And He gives us one primary job (knowing Him) that hinges on what we see as a weakness.

It's not a mistake. It's His design.

Follow me here: We must *know* God to do His work, and we must *experience* God's grace to really know Him, and we must *need* His grace to experience it. He made us needy so that we could accomplish what He wanted in only one way—*through Him.*

> *"My grace is sufficient for you,*
> *for my power is made perfect in weakness."*
>
> 2 CORINTHIANS 12:9 NIV

The Lord is eager and able to sweep your every mess out of the way so that you can take another step in your journey with Him. When you take the first leap and trust Him to do that, then you can deny Him nothing. Your heart is wide open, and your soul is forever linked to His—not because you're perfect, but because He won't have it any other way. Your weakness isn't an imperfection; it's a catalyst.

> *Create in me a clean heart, O God,*
> *and renew a steadfast spirit within me.*
> *Do not cast me away from Your presence,*
> *and do not take Your Holy Spirit from me.*
> *Restore to me the joy of Your salvation,*
> *and uphold me by Your generous Spirit.*

PSALM 51:10–12 NKJV

The amazing revelation is that if God had meant for me to do everything perfectly, by myself, He would have made me a little sturdier on my own. If He had meant for all of my faults and mistakes to follow me forever, as a weight around my heart, He would have prepared no relief. He would offer no grace. But He *does*.

He doesn't make us able to clean up the dust ourselves, but He makes us needy for the only fix there is. "Some trust in chariots and some in horses, but we trust in the name of the LORD our God" (Psalm 20:7 NIV).

And so that I would always remember to call on Him, He chose to make me the one thing I would have never picked for myself—vulnerable. I'm vulnerable to all of the forces that play on me in this world, to my weaknesses, to my imperfections, to my inferior wisdom; and I'm vulnerable to my own fruitless attempts at managing my life without Him. It's a weakness that answers to only one strength.

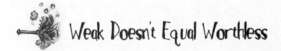 ## Weak Doesn't Equal Worthless

God sees how He made us, and He's not dissatisfied. He's not bothered with what we're lacking because we don't have to be perfect to do our work for Him, only committed and willing. What we see as flawed and fragile, God sees as capable and complete. His view is what matters.

To recognize my frame as part of God's plan is an enormous comfort. I don't have to be perfect—it's enough to want to be useful, to strive to be better, to keep trying in the face of setbacks. It's enough to reach out to God because I'm needy and weak and to trust that He will reach back. It's

His greatest joy when we turn to Him for help and guidance, salvation and forgiveness, when we surrender and ask Him to sweep our dust away.

The Lord made us imperfect and needy, and there's only one way we can ever understand why. We must replace the frustration with trust, the shame with gratitude. We can choose to believe that He knew what He was doing all along, and we can take the next step in our journey with Him in the lead. We can drop the dust at His feet and look into His heart instead.

* * * * *

Looking Through the Dust...

- In what areas of your life do you obsess about being perfect? How do you feel when you can't be perfect?
- Can you say, "Don't be so hard on yourself," to others far more easily than to yourself? What's the difference?

- Do others recognize your need for perfection? How do you explain it to them? To God?
- What work have you neglected or postponed because you felt too imperfect to do it? What would be a better step in your journey with God?

* * * * *

Lord, in Your grace, please help me past this obsession with my imperfections, and help me accept them instead and show them to You. Amen.

Chapter 3

How to Be Dust When You Want to Be Rock

*And in him you too
are being built together to become
a dwelling in which God lives by his Spirit.*

EPHESIANS 2:22 NIV

I don't know how many times I've wished to be as strong as rock! I imagine it's however many times that it didn't happen. I *want* to be tough and resilient and durable; but something always gets in the way, and that something is usually *me*. There I am, a pile of dust trying to become a mountain.

Do you know that feeling, trying to wade through piles of dust stronger than quicksand and deeper than guilt? It's like navigating your way through a briar patch, blind and unprotected. If you were a rock, it wouldn't hurt. But you're not, and the briar patch of failures and disappointments and confusion hurts badly.

I think I've run through that briar patch more than my fair share of times, and you may feel the same way, but that's not the point. It's not the briar patch that's the problem—it's the way we try to tread through it naked. We forget those coverings that the Lord wants to give us. But mostly, we think we should sew our own.

And oh, how we try! I can remember many times thinking that *this time, now,* I finally have it. I've read enough books, studied enough Scriptures, maybe even been good enough lately not to attract too much attention from above, that I can feel comfortable in the coverings I've created. I decide that I'll just accept my faults and problems and keep them all here in my little corner of the world, working on them when I can; and God can take care of someone who really deserves His care.

Do you know how ridiculous that sounds? The most generous, forgiving, loving Being *ever* wants to hold me in His hand, and I'm afraid to let Him. He offers to take all of those faults and problems from me; and instead, I say, "That's okay—really, I think I can handle it." If I came here as dust, well, I can handle that, too. I can mold my dust into a rock strong enough not to need anything.

Is that ever what happens? Well. . .no. Instead, I'm weak and fragile and vulnerable and needy and dependent. I try, and I fail. I dream dreams and set goals and then watch them shatter to the floor, unrealized. I doubt my abilities, my intellect, my compassion, and my reason for taking up space in this world. I fight the imperfect way I'm made with every ounce of energy I have. I can't even make it one day without a mistake with my feeble frame, and yet I think I should.

And as a river trying to flow uphill, I get nowhere. The river can't be a rock, and neither can I. We both have a path to follow, meandering perhaps with a few spills here and there, but always pulled by an unseen force to one destination.

The Lord isn't waiting at the gulf to judge the river's journey, and He isn't standing at the end of some to-do list waiting for us to appear with a string of good deeds we've accomplished on our own. He knows we'd never stand a chance, what with this weak frame spilling dust everywhere! So instead, in His grace, He walks with us, with a broom and a promise that we'll never walk alone.

> *Who is like the LORD our God,*
> *the One who sits enthroned on high,*
> *who stoops down to look on*
> *the heavens and the earth?*
> *He raises the poor from the dust and*
> *lifts the needy from the ash heap.*

PSALM 113:5–7 NIV

But we don't give up easily. I know the vain attempts well. Like a child in a pup tent in the backyard, a weak flashlight shining on a secret, *I'll do this and this and fix that and that while the Lord's not looking, and then maybe He'll think I'm not so terrible after all. I'll show Him that I'm not dust, that I can overcome these faults and correct these mistakes. I'll prove to Him that I'm worthy of His love. . . .*

We make these statements in our heads, and they hurt us in our hearts. Only with a willingness to accept God's grace can we ask for it. And time after time, we make that choice only as a last resort. And God says, "Where've you been?"

And we have to answer, "Well, I reckon I was lost somewhere in the do-it-yourself department. You been here all along?"

I Still Want to Be Rock

I bet God sometimes wonders how a pile of dust can be so stubborn! Like the same child who's stayed up deep into the night, I fall exhausted when I cannot, no matter how hard I try, get where I want to be on my own, without any mistakes. But with the strength of a river, I fight on, day after day.

I paddle, and I paddle, and the river seems to swallow me up. I wonder where all of my efforts are going and why I feel no relief from the past and no satisfaction with the present. I must look to God like a cloud trying to become a star or a leaf trying to become a raindrop.

He waits for me to stop, look at the deepening stream, and say, "Okay, I need a boat." With no way to lift myself from what threatens to consume me, I escape it only when I become less, not more.

You will keep in perfect peace him
whose mind is steadfast,
because he trusts in you.
Trust in the LORD forever,
for the LORD, the LORD, is the Rock eternal.

ISAIAH 26:3–4 NIV

Yet we just won't easily allow ourselves to see the part of the Lord's vision where He rescues and comforts us. Why *do* we fight the most gracious and benevolent of all plans? We fight it because we sometimes can't believe it's really true.

Why would God want to sweep up *my* dust? Why would He spend His obviously valuable time on *me*? Surely there's a catch. You have to be far better than I've been to *really* receive God's grace. . . .

Well, if you were that good, you wouldn't need it, now would you? I know how much you want to be the rock that never falters, strong and perfect. I also know that you can't. That's okay, because God can.

Knowing that we could do nothing for ourselves, God made Himself the rock we'd need from the beginning. Only one of us has to be the rock—either God or me. Now let's see. . .I wonder which of us is the better choice. . . ?

An unfathomable array of wonderful joys awaits us when we receive what the Lord is willing to give us, what is ours for the asking with a sincere heart. We may only be a pile of dust, but we can be a pile of dust that trusts in God's grace and goodness and unending love.

We can't ever overcome all of our human imperfections and clean up our messes by ourselves. We don't have to. Instead, the Lord will help us see how to drop all of our imperfections and mistakes and misjudgments into a pile that He can sweep away. He isn't looking for us to be perfect, only attentive and accepting of His protection and gifts. He doesn't want us to sew our own coverings, only to feel the warmth of the ones He's already made.

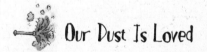 Our Dust Is Loved

For the Lord God is a sun and shield;
the Lord bestows favor and honor;
no good thing does he withhold from
those whose walk is blameless.

PSALM 84:11 NIV

Wow! Favor and honor from the Lord, all for me! These gifts He gives willingly to me and to you in our terribly dusty states, knowing that we need them and can never give them to ourselves. Ask, and He will keep "no good thing" from you; and what does He ask in return?

Not that we're perfect, lest we misunderstand. The charge is present tense and must be addressed and renewed as long as we live. To walk a walk "blameless" with Him is to walk a walk that never stops, even when we fail along the way. It's to walk now, today, not when we're "good enough." It's not a walk that ends when we spill a little dust (or even a lot of dust). It's not a walk that is dependent on *us* erasing all of our mistakes.

When we become "blameless," it is only because God has chosen to make us so, granting us redemption when we seek it. He doesn't make us perfect; He just bears the burden of our blame for us. Because He sweeps the piles of dust away, the path is clean. We can walk with Him safe and secure, knowing that our dust is never too much for Him. Our walk is now and eternal.

Our walk is also full of those wonderful gifts the Lord wants to give us, but there is an order. We cannot be blameless *before* we walk with

Him, and we cannot receive His gifts *before* we are blameless. Understand? Grace first, gifts next. You must ask for the boat *before* you can be rescued from the river. And through His inexplicable grace, He forgives our mistakes as if they never happened. He doesn't say, "This mess you've made I hold against you," but instead, "I've got it now. . . . Walk with Me."

Only when we kick our way through the dust—when we keep trying, going forward, with a sincere heart and total loyalty—can we use our otherwise worthless frame for its sole purpose: discipleship in whatever form the Lord intends. Despite the dusty trail we may leave through our efforts, God's focus is on the here and now. He sweeps up the dust, seals our cracks, and says, "Keep walking this way. I'm right here."

 He Can Handle It

And yet, we sometimes behave as if we have to make the journey all by ourselves, relying on our own sense of navigation. And at other times, we completely lose sight of the reason for the walk!

We get tired and depressed because we try to lead the way and end up going in circles. We pause and study the cracks here and there, walk in the dust we spill each day, and look to ourselves for a remedy and a road map. Guess that dust must have settled in our eyes. . . . It seems that we can see no farther than our last mistake.

Gripe, gripe, grumble, grumble. We go on and on, still cursing the dust and trying to deny it or sweep it ourselves when we should be looking to God. We can replace the "gripe, gripe, grumble, grumble" with "listen, listen, accept, accept," an approach that begins with asking for forgiveness so that we don't have to hide anything anymore.

When I kept silent, my bones wasted away
through my groaning all day long.
For day and night your hand was heavy upon me;
my strength was sapped as in the heat of summer.
Then I acknowledged my sin to you
and did not cover up my iniquity.
I said, "I will confess my transgressions
to the LORD"—and you
forgave the guilt of my sin.

PSALM 32:3–5 NIV

See? The Lord knows all about your dust (and mine). The "heavy hand" that you feel on you is heavy because it's so strong—strong enough to take whatever you've been hiding and call it His own. Then His hand is strong enough to make it disappear, completely and forever. Then His hand is strong enough to support your fragile frame while He walks that walk with you, every step of the way.

With a troubled and sincere heart, we can turn our attention from our weak frame to our impenetrable God. We can stop fighting. And when we give our dust to Him, we can then understand and take great comfort in these three truths:

The Lord's unfailing ability to be right and to use us as we are. Do you really want to question the Creator of all heaven and earth and declare that *you* would have done things better? I didn't think so.

God didn't make a mistake when He made us weak and dependent on Him. He didn't create and guarantee His grace and then stomp His foot and say, "Oh, no! I should have never made them *that* promise!" He didn't give us only one chance to get it right.

He didn't put us here in a sealed cage to keep in all of our mistakes and imperfections and keep out His love and forgiveness. He didn't give us a lifetime of work to do and then expect us to do it by ourselves. He didn't create us as a part of Himself and then decide that He would only accept us when we were "good enough."

He didn't breathe us to life only to let us smother in the dust that He *knew* we'd leak out now and then. *He didn't make any mistakes.* And He stands ready to help us get past ours so that we can get on with our work—yes, even you and me, standing in the dust piled higher than we are.

We have a calling to answer, and we can only hear it one way—not by being perfect and apart, but by being faithful and attached. " 'Remain in me, and I will remain in you. No branch can bear fruit by itself; it must remain in the vine. Neither can you bear fruit unless you remain in me. I am the vine; you are the branches. If a man remains in me and I in him, he will bear much fruit; apart from me you can do nothing' " (John 15:4–5 NIV).

The pattern hasn't changed. . . . All of us are made of dust and always will be. Even those people who you admire, those who have accomplished the most and reached the greatest heights, have done what they've done with a frame of dust just like yours and mine. They aren't "better" than you are or any more loved than you are. They've just learned where to go for the only help there is. They give their dust to God and let Him sweep it away.

If these people you revere look like mountains instead of sandpiles, it's because God sealed their cracks and built up layer upon layer of grace that repairs the deepest wounds. When someone is strong and courageous and productive, it's a strength and a power that comes only through the grout lines of her soul. A lack of grout doesn't mean perfection—it means a lack of redemption.

The Lord's grace and goodness, favor and love available to those blessed people you see is the same grace and goodness, favor and love available to *you*. Your dust is never strong enough to keep it away, and your deeds are never good enough to earn it— He's seen it all. And He's prepared. He is merciful and generous even to the likes of you and me. He takes our dust and makes us heirs.

But when the kindness and the love of God
our Savior toward man appeared,
not by works of righteousness which
we have done, but according to His mercy

*He saved us, through the washing of
regeneration and renewing of the Holy Spirit,
whom He poured out on us abundantly
through Jesus Christ our Savior,
that having been justified by His grace
we should become heirs
according to the hope of eternal life.*

TITUS 3:4–7 NKJV

What you have is all you need. You don't
need to be a mountain when you have God the
Rock to hold up your frame! You don't need to
be perfect, but you do need to *need*—grace,
understanding, love, direction. And all that you
need, God supplies, in unlimited quantities, in
perfect lines of grout to patch your frame.

You'll always have the same frame of dust and
you'll always make mistakes, but you won't be a
hopeless cause. You'll always be imperfect in this
life, but you'll be far from useless. God's grace
poured out on you abundantly is all you need—all
you need to get past the dust and take another step
in your journey with Him. With Him by your side
and no secrets or shame in between, you can do
whatever it is He has planned for you to do.

You can't use your dust as a reason to avoid your work, because the dust is always temporary. God's broom is all that's needed to sweep it away, and it's there for the asking. So when you focus more on His grace and your work and less on the dust, you'll see that you have all you need. Trust that the Lord will guide you in the work He wants you to do (what could a frame of dust do by itself anyway?) and will always, *always,* pick you up when you fall. Your failure isn't in making a misstep, but in refusing to trust those steps to God and to believe that He will still love you when you stumble.

To trust that He won't abandon us when we fail gives us amazing encouragement and inspiration to get back to serving Him. The belief that God has whatever we need in the most trying, frustrating, or challenging circumstance becomes a path of stone on which to plant our feet. The belief that He will grant His grace and sweep away our dust becomes a light that guides us on that path to blessings we can't even imagine. There is nothing more—only you and God, taking steps together, on your trust and His grace.

> *I will love You, O LORD, my strength.*
> *The Lord is my rock*
> *and my fortress and my deliverer;*
> *My God, my strength,*
> *in whom I will trust.*
>
> PSALM 18:1–2 NKJV

 Dust Isn't So Bad

Wishing to be a rock takes up a lot of time and energy. I should know because I've done it most of my life! Oh, sure, I've watched others overcome and carry on despite their dust, but I couldn't quite get there myself. So I propositioned God and tried to convince Him to make this one little change, this time, and just turn me into a rock that wasn't so fragile. Know what He said? "Dust isn't so bad."

I didn't like that answer very much, so I tried again. "Okay," I'd say, "if I have to be dust, please don't watch while I try to figure out how to deal with it, how about that?—" "Go ahead and try if you must. . . ," He said (knowing I had a better chance at time travel), "but dust isn't so bad."

He just wouldn't let it go! I want to be a

rock, and He defends the dust. I want to clean it up, and He says I can't. I can barely stand to admit it exists, and He says it's not so bad. Where does He get this stuff?

The Lord thinks and sees with His heart. The dust isn't so bad to Him because He knows it's temporary, innocuous. He sees the holes in our frame that He can patch in a heartbeat. He sees the dust and He sees *us*—fragile and loved and needy. He wants to clean and patch and watch us work.

You can take care of the dust your way or His way: He has a broom and you have a fan. He gathers and collects; you spread and scatter. Now, who do you think can round up the dust quicker and more efficiently?

But it doesn't start by wishing the dust away. It doesn't start by wishing to be a rock. It doesn't start by wishing for lighter burdens. It starts with seeking rest and solace. It starts when you say, "I can't do this my way anymore, Lord. Let's try Yours."

When we let our dust accumulate and overpower us, we are lost. When we look at it and ask the Lord to deal with it, we are found. And once found, the dust is irrelevant. All that matters is the grout that God uses to patch the holes in our frame—His unfailing grace.

Like traveling back or forward in time, trying to cover the cracks ourselves is hopeless. Our failures and mistakes and problems can't be *hidden from* God—they can only be *forgiven by* God. That's the only way we can ever come to terms with the dust, to let the Lord sweep it away. "He who covers his sins will not prosper, but whoever confesses and forsakes them will have mercy" (Proverbs 28:13 NKJV).

Hanging Out the Wash

An elderly neighbor who lives down the street from me stopped to talk one summer day. We stood at my front gate. She could see my laundry on the line in my backyard.

"You can't get any closer to God than hanging out your wash," she said in a quiet, Southern drawl.

It seemed like a rather odd comment, I thought at the time. I always loved to hang my wash on the line, but I had never thought of it as a spiritual practice before. The more I've considered what she said, though, the more I know she was absolutely right.

Aren't we a bit like the laundry, in need of attention for our stains and yet unable to cleanse ourselves? When we wash the clothes, they're still the same clothes, only clean and renewed, still useful and worthy of what they were designed for. When God grants His grace to us to sweep away our dust and mend our cracks, we're still the same souls, only clean and renewed, still useful and worthy of what we were designed for.

But there's one major difference (besides the obvious!) between us and the laundry. The clothes never resist our efforts to make them clean. They never form a committee in the hamper and decide to take that job upon themselves. They don't try to hide their dirt by folding themselves in such a way that it doesn't show.

And since we're about as good at cleaning ourselves as the clothes are, we stay stained until we are willing to ask for and accept God's grace, the grace that makes the stains disappear, that makes us blameless and new, that makes us ready to serve again. And His grace is enough for all your stains.

The dust we fear is not nearly as powerful as we might think it is. It's never more powerful than God. He can sweep it away no matter how far it's scattered or how deep it's buried or how nasty it is.

It's hard to believe, I know, but He made that promise long before you made a mistake. He said that we would become His "dwelling place." No worthless pile of dust can be a dwelling place of the Almighty—only a redeemed, patched, and loved pile of dust that looks to the Rock of God for help. The dust isn't so bad when you know where the broom is.

> *"Come to me, all you who are*
> *weary and burdened,*
> *and I will give you rest.*
> *Take my yoke upon you*
> *and learn from me,*
> *for I am gentle and humble in heart,*
> *and you will find rest for your souls."*
>
> MATTHEW 11:28–29 NIV

* * * * *

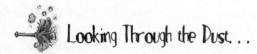 Looking Through the Dust...

- Why is it so hard to see yourself the way the Lord sees you, "blameless"?

- What kind of walk have you been walking with God up to now? As a blameless child of God, how can your walk be changed?
- When you're safely in the boat, what will you do with the gift of God's grace?
- Show the Lord your messiest dust. Write down what He says. How can you be like the laundry today?

* * * * *

Lord, in Your grace, please help me to see that Your forgiveness makes the dust of my life manageable, that Your strength makes my weakness irrelevant. Amen.

 **Chapter 4**

Preparing For Cleanup

The LORD is near to all who call upon Him,
to all who call upon Him in truth. He will
fulfill the desire of those who fear Him;
He also will hear their cry and save them.

PSALM 145:18–19 NKJV

God is so prepared. Any time of the day or night that we approach Him, what does He say? "Sorry, I can't talk to you right now; gimme a minute. . . ." Hardly. He is there because He can be nowhere else. He is prepared for us because He can be no other way. He is eager to extend to us His grace because He isn't worried about our imperfections, even when we are. He's always prepared to start anew today, with whatever we're willing to give Him. It's a trait we can trust.

In him and through faith in him
we may approach God
with freedom and confidence.

EPHESIANS 3:12 NIV

We can't ever prepare enough to foresee or circumvent every misstep we'll make, but we can prepare ourselves to accept the Lord's abundant grace. He won't force it on you, but He will also never withhold it from you. He waits for your attitude to become more like His. You can prepare for the sweeping of your dust when you have an *attitude* of acceptance—the willingness to trust God's grace and the humility to receive it.

The Right View, the Right Attitude

If we depend on our view of ourselves to overcome our dust, we'll never get there. What we see is what the human mind sees: mistakes that can't be forgiven, problems that never go away, dreams unfulfilled, hopes disintegrated. What an awful mess we see everywhere!

But it's not a *permanent* mess. The dust changes

74

when our view changes. Consider how God sees you and me. He's seen us as forgiven and accepted and included and loved since before we were born.

Granting His grace to us and forgiving us our flaws isn't something that occurred to Him after a few million of us had made some mistakes. He made our need for His grace even before He made us. It was a part He could no doubt have changed, but He didn't. He made us this way, vulnerable as dust; and at the same time, He prepared for our redemption.

For he chose us in him before the creation of the world to be holy and blameless in his sight. In love he predestined us to be adopted as his sons through Jesus Christ, in accordance with his pleasure and will.

EPHESIANS 1:4–5 NIV

He made you holy and blameless in *His* sight—so who are you to argue? *Well, I'm certainly not holy and blameless,* you say. Me, neither. At least, we're not holy and blameless in the human way we tend to think of it. But remember, the Lord sees differently.

Remember the blameless walk that He desires from us (Psalm 84:11 NIV)? That walk is the total dependence on God, the absence of any self-serving pride or misunderstood duty. It is the same here. We have a hard time understanding that, but let's try.

Holy and blameless don't mean an earthly perfection (like we wish we had) but forgiven by God's grace when we ask (which is all we need). All of the blame disappears in His sight, and what is left is a devotion unmatched and perfect to the God who is great enough to clean up even the biggest mess we make. We can't see what He sees when all we see is our own shame and efforts to cover it up.

We are holy and blameless when we are devoted and humble, trusting God for what we need instead of trying to manufacture it ourselves. We are holy and blameless when we make the choice to say, "Father, here I am," when we listen for the answer we trust will come from a God who freely gives grace to the undeserving.

And we are an undeserving bunch! We always will be; but if we focus on our mistakes and failures instead of God's view, we'll never see the love and peace that is ours for the asking. We'll always see ourselves as the sorrowful child hiding in her closet trying to tape up the lamp she just broke. With a view full of her own efforts, she can't see the help that lives nearby.

The Lord could snatch us up in His hand and shake at us all the lamps we've broken if He wanted to. He could keep a record of every fracture for all eternity. He could see us any way He chooses, remind us incessantly of how often we fail, and stand over us with an embarrassingly long list of our flaws. He could do that easily enough, but He doesn't.

Through His grace and the capacity that only He has, He knows our imperfections and loves us anyway. He even invites us into His kingdom. He accepts us as the ancient families accepted slaves, who, when adopted by their masters, were granted the same privileges as a natural-born child.

Amazing! The Lord stands ready to grant me that kind of grace; and instead I step back, ashamed of my need and wanting to wait until I've filled it myself to go to Him? That's just another example of our distorted vision. We should look elsewhere.

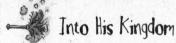
Into His Kingdom

The slave of the Roman Empire could never achieve the status of a natural-born child on his own. And we can never achieve enough to make God say, "Well, look at her! I think I'd like to adopt her into my family because she's so good!" Sounds ridiculous, I know, but we do it all the time.

A Roman slave couldn't change his ancestry, and we can't change our imperfections. But we can ask God to accept us *anyway.* We can ask Him to help us get up when we fall *anyway.* We can ask Him to sweep up the dust we leave in our wake *anyway.* We can ask for His grace *anyway.* And He gives it, not because of our efforts or performance, but because it is His "pleasure and will." And He asks for one thing first: *the right attitude.*

> *He mocks proud mockers but*
> *gives grace to the humble.*
>
> PROVERBS 3:34 NIV

Do you see what that says? God gives grace "to the humble," not to the perfect who don't exist, not to those who think they're perfect and don't need it, not to those who are too ashamed to ask for it—but to those who are *humble* in their approach. No other requirement is mentioned. The grace does not go to those who are humble and not quite so bad, or to those who are humble and close to perfection, or to those who are humble and have done great things. It goes to those who are humble enough to ask and receive.

Your humility is part of the *personal* relationship that God wants with you. When you approach Him in a humble manner, you are ready to accept what He gives, not before. And you never have to be afraid to ask, afraid of the all-powerful Lord who can do as He wishes. " 'Do not fear, little flock, for it is your Father's good pleasure to give you the kingdom' " (Luke 12:32 NKJV).

 Developing the Attitude of Grace

The humility that the Lord wants you to have isn't a weak or fearful humility. It is one based on the promises He's already made and your faith that He will honor them. Your attitude about God's grace defines how you will accept it and allow it to work in your life. It has nothing to do with God's ability to extend it to you, but it has everything to do with your willingness to claim it as your own.

There are five parts to developing the *attitude of grace*. Let's look at them one at a time:

1. Happily accept your need. When you decide to prepare yourself for the wonderful cleansing of the Lord, you can do it in complete confidence that He will answer your prayers. He has already accepted everything about you and knows exactly what you need. Be grateful that you can accept yourself, too, and know that there is a place to go for what you need now and what you will forever need in the future.

Let us therefore come boldly to the throne of grace,
that we may obtain mercy and
find grace to help in time of need.

HEBREWS 4:16 NKJV

2. Show it to God. Once you have decided to accept your need, you can't stop there. You and the Lord have to talk about it and come to terms with it. You have to be able to go to Him and show Him everything that hurts. You can't keep any secrets. You can't hide your hurts in the darkness because they will only go away when you expose them to God's light. And when you're in His light, you can see so much better! You can see that there's no need to keep anything from Him. You can see past the dust pile and through the pain to the place He wants you to be.

> *If we say that we have fellowship with Him,*
> *and walk in darkness,*
> *we lie and do not practice the truth.*
> *But if we walk in the light as*
> *He is in the light, we have fellowship*
> *with one another, and the*
> *blood of Jesus Christ His Son cleanses*
> *us from all sin.*

1 JOHN 1:6–7 NKJV

3. Rejoice and stand in God's grace. Realize what you've been given when you go to God and He grants you this immortal gift. Realize what He bestows upon you with the first breath you utter, "Please, Lord. . ." Realize that His grace surrounds you and sustains you, that "this grace in which we stand" isn't going anywhere. Once He gives you this beautiful gift, it is yours to keep. Stand on it forever, and it will never shift. Cling to it daily, and it will never fade. Rejoice in it because it's yours.

> *Therefore, having been justified by faith,*
> *we have peace with God through*
> *our Lord Jesus Christ, through whom also*
> *we have access by faith into*
> *this grace in which we stand,*
> *and rejoice in hope of the glory of God.*
>
> ROMANS 5:1–2 NKJV

4. Work anyway. The gift of God's grace shapes the way we look at our world. There is more hope and peace, more faith and forgiveness, but we still fail. God's grace doesn't make us perfect. It makes us useful. Even though we still make mistakes and still fall short of all that we believe we should be in the life God's planned for us, we can still work. We can find whatever is within us and use it. We can stand firm and be the disciple the Lord needs, warts and all. The responsibility remains.

Therefore, my dear brothers, stand firm.
Let nothing move you.
Always give yourselves fully to the work
of the Lord, because you
know that your labor in the Lord
is not in vain.

1 CORINTHIANS 15:58 NIV

5. Keep trusting, and keep growing. Working in God's grace is a brave new adventure. It's full of surprises and challenges. Sometimes, we might feel that we've fallen out of the boat we need to keep us safe, but that never happens. Regardless of our failures in the past, the Lord still wants us to be brave and creative, bold and secure, to trust that He will never leave us alone for one instant. We are His heirs, and He deserves our trust. The power and the promise of this life you've been given is waiting, and He stands ready to help you accomplish your dreams. The best is yet to be.

Now this is the confidence that we
have in Him,
that if we ask anything according
to His will, He hears us.

1 JOHN 5:14 NKJV

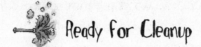

Ready for Cleanup

God only looks at your future because He's canceled out your past. You can do the same when you seek and accept His grace. Allow yourself to believe that He has forgiven you what you've asked of Him, that He understands better than you think, and that He loves you enough to guide you through whatever happens next.

How could the Lord ever leave you alone to deal with your cleanup? " 'I am the good shepherd; and I know My sheep,' " (John 10:14 NKJV) Jesus said. I'm not about to question the depth of His knowledge! I only need to make sure that my attitude is right. He goes on to tell me: " 'If you abide in Me, and My words abide in you, you will ask what you desire, and it shall be done for you' " (John 15:7 NKJV).

When I approach the Lord with confidence and reverence, when I give Him this life He's given me, when I trust in His generosity and perfection, then I need only desire one thing, and all else will be done. I ask for His grace; and everything that follows, if I accept it, is the beautiful and exquisite unfolding of the "unsearchable riches of Christ" into *my* undeserving time on earth.

How amazing is that! Your *attitude* is your first step toward your acceptance of God's grace. He stands waiting and willing. You decide when this wonderful adventure begins. Yes, it means looking at the dust around you; but that's where all good cleanups start, with acceptance of the mess. And how blessed we are—the Lord stands there with a broom! It's unlike any we've ever imagined, powerful enough even for *us*.

To begin your adventure, go to God with your dust in your hands, trust Him to sweep your past aside, and look for the wonder that is yet to come. Then you can rest upon His grace so that your imperfection doesn't hurt anymore, so that something more important takes center stage. Then you can get beyond those irrational yet deeply ingrained and unrealistic expectations of yourself so that you can use what you have for the work you have to do.

The Lord's grace is the ultimate guide to self-help, to making better choices, improving yourself, and dealing with your flaws. It's not a ticket to perfection, but a way to work with what you have.

Don't you want to know what's possible when God's grace is a part of your life? Don't you want to go where He's planned for you to go? The baggage of the past won't let you unless you give it to God to sweep away. Your shabby frame can't carry you forward until you let Him patch the cracks. You can't see what awaits until you adopt an *attitude of grace* so that He can move the piles of dust out of your way and repair and prepare you for wonders to come. Then the show begins!

> *"Call to Me, and I will answer you,*
> *and show you great and mighty*
> *things, which you do not know."*
>
> JEREMIAH 33:3 NKJV

* * * * *

 Looking Through the Dust...

- What view of yourself have you had lately? Is it a human view or a godly view?

- Can you understand *God's* attitude of His grace? How can you make it your own?
- How have you been approaching God, in humility or some other way? How can you improve your approach?
- Can you apply the five parts of an *attitude of grace* to your life today? Which will be the hardest for you?

* * * * *

Lord, in Your grace, *please help me to humbly come to You broken and dusty, to accept Your love and forgiveness, and to prepare for a future of purpose. Amen.*

Part 2

"Maybe a Vacuum Cleaner Would Be Better?"

The *Application* of God's Grace

Blessed is he whose transgressions are forgiven,
whose sins are covered. Blessed is the man
whose sin the LORD does not count against him
and in whose spirit is no deceit.

PSALM 32:1–2 NIV

"I gotta tell You, Lord. There's a lot of dust piled up here. Have You looked lately? And the pile keeps growing, like cobwebs in a dark corner. As hard as I try to seal the cracks, this faulty frame of mine still spills out dust like goodies from a Christmas stocking. Only it's not good stuff; it's bad stuff. I fail and I get angry and I make mistakes and I hurt others. There's another crack in my frame and a new pile of dust every day. Now what are You gonna do about that?"

"Patch the cracks and sweep the dust away. Any questions?"

"Well, yeah, I have a few hundred questions."

"Only My question really matters, you know."

"Your question?"

"Yes, My question and your answer. I never change, remember. The question is, are you ready to?"

"That's it? *Am I ready to change?*"

"My grace is transforming, all that you need. You must come to Me with your heart open and ready to receive not just forgiveness, but blessings, too. I can't do that part for you. I ask again, are you ready to change? Are you ready for this transformation?"

"More than ready! Will You help me?"

"You have to ask? That's My job! And like I said, I never change."

* * * * *

90

Chapter 5

Overcoming an Unchangeable Past

The LORD will fulfill his purpose for me; your love, O LORD, endures forever—do not abandon the works of your hands.

PSALM 138:8 NIV

You know those little cartoon characters who tiptoe, all bent over and petrified as they walk through a scary place, and their shadow looms behind them, about a hundred times bigger than they are and somehow displays a menacing look of its own? The little character slips around corners and down long hallways, and the shadow always remains, ever so close.

Then the horrified little creature suddenly sees a mirror, and the reflection that stares back at him is the big, bad shadow that scares him worse than whatever he was trying to avoid in the first place. He jumps to the ceiling, screams a celluloid scream, and tears out of there, colorful swoosh marks trailing him all the way. It's a funny sight, and sometimes we look *exactly* the same. We grant great power to our past, and the shadow that follows us is bigger than we are. Do you really want to live your life like a cartoon character? Me, neither.

The past is unchangeable, but it's not unforgivable; and release from it is not unreachable (even when we think it is), because of God's power and grace. The change that He talks about begins in *us*, not Him. He's made that rather clear. And if the Lord could breathe a universe into being, surely He could do something with our past, don't you think?

It's a tough idea to swallow sometimes, though. I know the feeling. The cartoon-size shadow I've seen behind myself a few times was more than my weak frame could hold off, and it was filled with all kinds of dust. I made the pile myself, the one that morphed into something big and ugly, that took on a life built from the past, that wanted to control my present and my future.

As horrifying as that shadow is, trying to escape it seems so much safer than finally looking at the mess and seeing it for what it is: the history of an imperfect life, not the prediction of a doomed future. We see an enormous mountain that we cannot change. Yet what looks like it would take a turbocharged vacuum cleaner to clean up, God treats like only a speck, fodder even for something better.

What some sturdy straws His broom must have to deal with an ugly past and a weak disciple! Perfect is nowhere to be found, but He doesn't look for it. He looks for an answer to His question, for me to be ready to apply His grace to my life. And with my long overdue answer, we begin to overcome an unchangeable past.

Do not conform any longer to the
pattern of this world,
but be transformed by the renewing of your mind.
Then you will be able to test and approve
what God's will is—
his good, pleasing and perfect will.

ROMANS 12:2 NIV

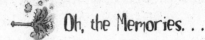

Oh, the Memories. . .

Sometimes, a memory is a wonderful thing. We can recall great joy and tremendous blessings, times when we felt the hand of God and sat in the lap of His riches. But there's a flip side. There always is....

That same memory records regretted deeds and abandoned hopes, words of hate and thoughts of vileness that we wish had never been. We remember the distance we've put between us and the Lord, the stupid choices and unrighted wrongs of our past. We remember all too well. *What was I thinking?!* we scream inside our heads.

And those unwanted piles of dust in your memory will bury everything else if you're not careful. The imperfect gets pushier and grabs you by your thoughts and says, "Hey, look at me, it's your fault I'm here!" Even the best of the best is no match for the best of the worst, and your mind spends more time in the past than any-where else. Why do we do that to ourselves?

Of all our imperfections, why can't a poor memory be one of them when we want it to be?! I only have one answer for that—because we don't need one. It's *the Lord's* memory that matters, and His is quite selective.

> Remember, O LORD, your great mercy and love,
>   for they are from of old.
> Remember not the sins of my youth
>   and my rebellious ways;
> according to your love remember me,
>   for you are good, O LORD.

PSALM 25:6–7 NIV

When we're finally ready to let God take care of the past and begin that transformation He talks about, we can be like David the psalmist and revel in His grace. That transforming grace allows God to find us *right now* and to forget our past *right now.* God's grace makes this imperfect life perfect for what He has in mind. It's just a fact that rests on the never-changing God.

Overcoming, Coming Over

Everything that we drag around from our past puts that much more weight on this frame of dust that we have to live in today. Everything that we keep for ourselves that could be given to God pokes holes in that frame and spills dust everywhere as long as we hold on to it. Everything wonderful in this life that awaits us is waiting on only one thing: for us to decide that we want to claim it.

> *Let the wicked forsake his way,*
> *and the unrighteous man his thoughts;*
> *let him return to the LORD,*
> *and He will have mercy on him;*
> *and to our God,*
> *for He will abundantly pardon.*

ISAIAH 55:7 NKJV

Hmm, must have put that "abundantly" in there for me! That's not the most important part, though. It's the first part, the part where we "return to the Lord."

It's when we make that choice to leave the past in the past, and when we decide not to repeat it, that we can bathe in God's mercy. With one simple step from us, we can count on His pardon without end. We can trust in the fact of God's *character*, in the depth of His *mercy*, and in the strength of His *power*. Then we can rest in the marvel of His *wonder*. And then we can apply His indescribable gift to our lives.

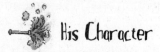 His Character

*Let us draw near to God with a sincere
heart in full assurance of faith,
having our hearts sprinkled to cleanse us
from a guilty conscience and
having our bodies washed with pure water.
Let us hold unswervingly
to the hope we profess, for he who
promised is faithful.*

HEBREWS 10:22–23 NIV

God is faithful even when we aren't, forgiving even when we are punishing. He's there to cleanse and redeem us, waiting on us to answer His question. He never moves beyond a breath away, and He is never slow to share His gifts. With "full assurance of faith," we can cling to the God who doesn't change so that we can.

While God has never had to deal with a

"guilty conscience," we certainly have! I have cried over mistakes lots of times and wallowed in my own disgust. Dare I hope for grace with all the dusty baggage I'm carrying? I think not. Then again. . .God never requires a perfect frame, but a *sincere heart.* I have that! I have a heart without malice, confident in His character even when mine is questionable.

 His Mercy

Have mercy on me, O God,
according to your unfailing love;
according to your great compassion
blot out my transgressions.
Wash away all my iniquity and
cleanse me from my sin.

PSALM 51:1–2 NIV

God's mercy is unending, a gift that cannot be understood with the logic we try to apply to it. When we're holding the weight of our past in front of our hearts, we wonder why a perfect God would grant forgiveness to anything as imperfect as we are. We look for a reason based on merit or stature. He doesn't have to.

While God's grace obliterates our dust pile, His mercy is warm and comforting, like wool on a lamb. Grace transforms; mercy envelops. Grace without mercy would be extortion, given out of greed instead of love. God wraps us in a cover of His mercy that creates us functional and useful again. He looks for the potential in us and cleanses everything that we've contaminated with an easy stroke. Then we have a beautiful top coat that prepares us for the world. God doesn't punish us for what lies beneath. He banishes the dust far, far away, and His mercy remains.

He has not dealt with us according to our sins,
nor punished us according to our iniquities.
For as the heavens are high above the earth,
so great is His mercy toward those who fear Him;
as far as the east is from the west,
so far has He removed our transgressions from us.

PSALM 103:10–12 NKJV

If He dealt with us "according to our sins," we'd wear our past on the outside, like a lamb turned inside out. There would be no top coat of protection thick enough to cover everything we'd have to expose. But that's not what happens. His mercy is too deep, and we are too loved.

 His Power

Because the past is too much for us to handle doesn't mean that it's too much for the Lord to handle. He can breathe His grace upon it and let it touch us no more, no matter what, wherever we are, because "surely the arm of the LORD is not too short to save, nor his ear too dull to hear" (Isaiah 59:1 NIV).

This power God has is stronger than the farthest thing your mind can imagine, and yet it hinges on your belief in it. Even though your mind can't comprehend such power, your heart must treat it like the most natural thing in the world. What your heart accepts, your mind believes. The result is the journey back to God. Sometimes it's the belief in the improbable that gets us through the impossible.

And if they do not persist in unbelief,
they will be grafted in,
for God is able to graft them in again.

ROMANS 11:23 NIV

It's a journey *back,* because any detours we've made have been a result of our own navigations. But whenever we manage to lose ourselves, God's power is strong enough to get us back to Him. He is no doubt forever able to graft us in *again.* There is a wound where we broke away, but it can be healed by the God who holds the greatest power in the world.

His Wonder

When we decide to begin this journey back to God, we think about His grace and we're grateful. We think about our past and we're sorry. We think about our present and we're nervous. We think about our future and we're fearful. What happens if we are able to get past the past? Then what? Glad you asked. The wonders await. . . .

Be renewed in the spirit of your mind,
and that you put on the new man
which was created according to God,
in true righteousness and holiness.

EPHESIANS 4:23–24 NKJV

The Lord never wastes anything. He will take everything old and create for you something new. He will take everything that hurts and banish it with His healing. He will take everything you've squandered and turn it into something you can use. The wonder of His ways will amaze you.

Because God's grace is transforming, you can see what it does to you. You can feel the effects of a heart that the Lord has healed. You can look in the mirror and see not a frightening shadow of the past, but the redeemed soul of a daughter of God. And the reflection will go deeper than the skin you see, all the way to your heart and spirit.

I will give you a new heart and
put a new spirit in you;
I will remove from you your heart of stone
and give you a heart of flesh.

And I will put my Spirit in you and
move you to follow my decrees
and be careful to keep my laws.

EZEKIEL 36:26–27 NIV

When you are ready to leave the past behind—whatever it is—God is ready to transform your heart, making it receptive and responsive to His ways. If we believe that the Lord will grant His grace to us, the undeserving, we must go farther and believe that He will provide us instruction and comfort, guidance and courage so that our walk with Him is more about the work He has for us and less about the pain with which we've paved the way thus far.

The wonder is that God's gifts don't end with His grace. They begin to blossom in us, increasing tenfold with every heartbeat, because our mind is fixed on Him, and His mind has forgotten the past. Our heart and our spirit can only follow where He leads into a future of wonder, because "to each one of us grace has been given as Christ apportioned it" (Ephesians 4:7 NIV).

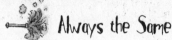 ## Always the Same

Remember that God made us needy for Him. He knows that we will need His grace continually as we struggle in this world. We'll always be imperfect, but we begin to truly escape from the past when we look to Him for the only sanctuary there is.

Even if we could become perfect from this day forward, that wouldn't change what has happened before. Even if we were frozen right now like an icicle, we would still have the same unchangeable past. We can never undo what we've done or relive what we've lived. We can't put our dust in one of those machines that splits atoms and blow it into space so far that we can't see it. But we can do something much more effective. We can take these feeble frames to a place of acceptance and rest, an eternal home where we are always invited in, where the shadows are never big and scary.

> *"The grass withers, the flower fades,*
> *but the word of our God*
> *stands forever."*

ISAIAH 40:8 NKJV

We overcome an unchangeable past with an unchangeable God.

How could something so simple seem so complicated? The failure, the sorrow, and the regret that we see as dust, God sees as gone like the grass, faded like the flower. And He's there forever to help us see it, too, when we answer His question, when we apply what He gives freely to our lives that could never exhaust His supply. Ahh, finally. . . a chance to overcome the past.

* * * * *

 Sweeping Away the Dust. . .

- Are you ready for the transformation that God promises? What is your answer to His question?
- How close is the shadow of the past behind you? Will you accept God's offer to shrink it with His grace?
- Will you let yourself rest in the safety of God's mercy and believe in the wonders He has yet to show you?
- Can you choose *today* to let go of your past

and begin to learn how to apply God's grace to your life?

* * * * *

Lord, by Your grace, *I can leave the past that hurts and rest on Your love that heals. Please touch me with Your mercy and transform me continually into the disciple You need me to be. Amen.*

Chapter 6

Transforming Failure into Trust

Trust in the LORD with all your heart,
and lean not on your own understanding;
In all your ways acknowledge Him,
and He shall direct your paths.

PROVERBS 3:5–6 NKJV

Sometimes I feel like I stack up all my failures and take roll call every night. I keep them close through the darkness and then, in the daylight, hang each disappointment around my neck like a tree trunk. While the failures are already killing me, I go ahead and start each day fully expecting to only add to their weight as I go. The only trust I can feel is the trust in my own likelihood of imperfection, and it screams at me nonstop. There is no relief.

Do you know that feeling? It hurts! Carrying around all my failures is like carrying around a rattlesnake. I can't make a move because I'm afraid of another mistake and more pain. There's no transformation because I'm paralyzed with fear. And yet, I cannot stop. The world demands that I go on, clumsy and dusty as ever. There is no time to whine. There is so much that I have to do and ample opportunity to fail. . . .

What a horrible way to look at the future! And yet, we do it all the time, don't we? We overlook anything positive and focus squarely on the less than perfect (which is everything). And when that happens, it's hard to trust in God or ourselves.

Yet, my quest for perfection continues, disappointing toil that it is. I fail to succeed—perfectly. I fail to act—godly. I fail to love —enough. And all I can see is the list with no check marks, no evidence that I've accomplished anything (whether it's true or not). I know you understand. And we let all of these failures that we focus on every day keep us from God. It seems so backward; but until we choose to reclaim the peace and joy and redemption that only He gives, we miss the point completely.

Frustrated and ashamed about everywhere

we fail, we begin to wonder *why* we fail so much when we *do* try as hard as we can. There could be tons of reasons why all of our efforts don't succeed, but we focus on a few out of desperation. Has God abandoned us? Has He decided to withhold His guidance and instruction? Has He forgotten about our needs and our plans? Has He become as obsessed with our failures as we have? No, He's done none of that. There's only one failure He's worried about.

Our failure to trust that He is *still in control* has become our biggest failure of all, and it's the only one that matters. When we have no trust, we have a lifetime of futile, everyday human failures that teach us nothing. We have forgotten "that what He had promised He was also able to perform" (Romans 4:21 NKJV), but we can change that. We can transform the failure into trust, one step at a time.

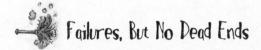 ## Failures, But No Dead Ends

I know what you're thinking: "How can I change the failure into anything? It's already done!"

You're right, in one way. Some failures are real acts that you can't deny or redo (we'll talk about the three kinds of failure in a moment), but God is waiting for you to change your interpretation of your failures and what comes with them.

Your failures can destroy you when you let their testimony of imperfection shout louder than anything else. Or they can be part of your journey in God's grace if you'll trust in Him to work them into your imperfect life and to never let them keep you from Him. His grace is that strong.

Despite any failure, you can rest in God's grace because He can still use everything you have and everything you are to work His plan—if you'll entrust it to Him.

> *"I have been crucified with Christ;*
> *it is no longer I who live,*
> *but Christ lives in me; and the life*
> *which I now live in the flesh*
> *I live by faith in the Son of God,*
> *who loved me and gave Himself for me."*
>
> GALATIANS 2:20 NKJV

Making that commitment to trust every day is hard, isn't it? It's especially hard when we think,

I've done my very best and still failed. It's not fair!
That's another one of our human emotions that
the Lord endures while He knows, "It's not what
looks fair in her mind that troubles her. It's the
trust in her heart that's missing."

The kind of success and fairness we're looking for isn't necessarily what God's most concerned about. We want results: "Please, let this
work this time!" And He wants a relationship:
"Please, walk with Me now and forever!"

 Building Every Day

As part of His unfathomable grace, He promises
us His companionship while we are becoming
that dwelling in which "God lives by His Spirit."
He's focused on moving in with us; then He'll
worry about where we're going. All of the failures
you have are just scaffolding, not to be hidden,
but to be used as you go about growing that relationship with the Lord.

To build a dwelling place for God is to trust
that He wants to live in such an imperfect place,
that the failures won't scare Him away or reveal

a weak side of you that His grace can't support.

He understands our never-ending struggle. Every day, we try, we fail, we try again; then we succeed at something or we abandon it. The tragedy is not in our failures, and the beauty is not in our successes. The reason for it all is the building process, when we choose to learn and dare to trust. The wonderful transformation of failure into trust works with all three kinds of failure, and it always begins with a new view.

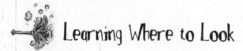 ## Learning Where to Look

In You, O LORD, I put my trust;
let me never be ashamed;
deliver me in Your righteousness.
Bow down Your ear to me,
deliver me speedily; be my rock of refuge,
a fortress of defense to save me.

PSALM 31:1–2 NKJV

It's always embarrassing to have to admit a failure. Whether it's to our family, our friends, our coworkers, ourselves—it doesn't matter. When we fail, it's like wearing a big sign that advertises our imperfections to everyone.

"Look at me—again—I've failed!" my mind and my face have screamed to all who would listen even when my heart wanted so desperately to conceal the defeats. But when the failures are a part of your life, you can't hide them. It's like trying to deny you have feet when you walk and just as pointless.

We must learn a new way to look at our failures. It isn't easy, because we'd rather not look at them at all! But much of our building is *study,* not doing but *learning.* And we must let go of what shames and frustrates us so that God can use it all. He will not be afraid of any failure you have. In fact, He's already got a plan for it.

If you have to start slowly, that's okay. Lay your failures out there for Him to see and trust in His grace a split second. He won't waste the opportunity while you're at His knee. Believe that He will "bow down" to wherever you are— even in that lowly place where you live when you exalt your failures higher than God's grace. He'll snatch up those failures you're so worried about, and watch where He'll put them—into His "transformational tool kit."

He'll put them there because He can *use* them. Your one second of trust transforms painful failures into instruments of instruction. It's the chance the Lord's been waiting for. When you're ready to admit and abandon your failures to God, then you can grasp His Spirit that is ready to help you build anew. Look at the Lord, not at your failures. The change of view is just what your heart needs.

 A View in Peace

"You will keep him in perfect peace,
whose mind is stayed on You,
because he trusts in You."

ISAIAH 26:3 NKJV

When you trust for that second, whether you know it or not, a beautiful thing happens. You make a very lucrative trade with the Lord. Staring at the dust piles won't ever calm your mind and give rest to your soul. Analyzing your failures over and over won't create a peace in you because you're not capable of doing that for yourself. Only a God who has never failed can comfort you in your failures. If you want to experience His bountiful grace, you have to make a trade—your failure for His peace. It's amazing what trust in the right place can do!

Look into God's heart and look away from the failure. Reflected there you will see what to take from the failure and how to apply it to your life. Give the past and the future to God, and He'll give His peace to you right now. He'll never abuse your trust.

And once in the security of His heart, where He loves you no matter what, you will begin to learn what to do with the failures of your life, those done and those to come.

Then, in His peace, we can get past our failures in our imperfect but God-directed way because, like a good parent, He is constantly "training us up in the way we should go" (see Proverbs 22:6). We need only trust that He will clear that way for us and help us with the navigation. Every step "in the way we should go" is one step in the transformation from perfect failure to imperfect but trusting growth, and that's perfect enough.

For You will light my lamp;
the LORD my God will enlighten my darkness.
For by You I can run against a troop,
by my God I can leap over a wall.
As for God, His way is perfect;
the word of the LORD is proven;
He is a shield to all who trust in Him.
For who is God, except the LORD?
And who is a rock, except our God?
It is God who arms me with strength,
and makes my way perfect.

PSALM 18:28–32 NKJV

Will we learn quickly to leap over that wall that's in front of us? Well, you might, but I never have. Some of us (me) take awhile. It's not been because the Lord's a poor teacher, but because I've been reluctant to trust in His grace when the failures blocked my view, afraid to believe that all He needed was my willingness to change.

On the blessed occasions when I *would* trust enough and let Him see my heart, I was amazed at how gentle He was. All of my work became study instead of toil, not in search of an end that I conceived, but in an aura of peace that only He could provide. There was no need to be perfect, just the willingness not to be overwhelmed with my heavy failures, all three kinds: those *finished, unfinished,* and *misunderstood.* Maybe you can relate.

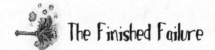 The Finished Failure

This kind of failure may be the most depressing of all because it is a fact of your life that cannot be changed. It's the easiest kind to identify and possibly the hardest to accept. This is losing a business, ending a marriage, missing an opportunity that will not pass this way again. These failures are big ones that hurt for a long time. We can't get away from them because they help to define who we are, whether we like it or not.

We don't usually have many of these major failures, and it's a good thing! They're tough to handle, and we always give them too much power. With these big failures, we decide that we'll never get anywhere even *close* to perfect, and we seal our fate with mistakes of the past that even God cannot undo. But these finished failures are still not big enough to hide us from God's grace.

*The LORD redeems the soul of His servants,
and none of those who
trust in Him shall be condemned.*

PSALM 34:22 NKJV

What God cannot change about your past failures, He uses to teach for the present and bank for the future. All He needs is your trust that He knows how to take a mess and bless it into something else. Trust in that, and you can get past the past.

Your trust in the Lord says that He is bigger than your biggest mistake. And if you believe that, then you have to believe that He will help you, redeem you, and comfort you when the pain of your past is strong. Remembering God's attitude toward your imperfections will help improve your own.

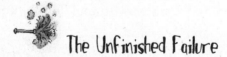

The Unfinished Failure

These are the failures that drag you down like an undertow in a hurricane. They include the failure to be the kind of friend you want to be or the failure to carry through with a dream or the failure to live your life for God. Because we're always going to be imperfect, this kind of failure keeps coming back, like hiccups and crabgrass. Struggling with these can become an agonizing battle—an extra big club to whack yourself with now and then. I've done it for years now with an unfinished failure that haunts me, the constant worry that I'm failing to be the mom I should be.

I can remember many times when I made a list in my tired mind of all the ways I've failed my son. I've thought about every misspoken word, every irrational decision, every poor choice that's hurt him. I want to be the perfect mom, to never fail him, to never make a mistake. It hasn't turned out that way.

But God has not abandoned me with this failure. When I've given Him a moment of trust, He has been there to help me see that this fatalistic view I have can change. I can trade in this unfinished failure to God and receive His grace, then trust that He will help me change the present and the future into something wonderful. My son is still here, and the Lord will not expect me to do this most important job alone. I have to trust in that even when it's easier not to.

God will not fail to portion out His grace to

me and help me be the better parent I need to be. Perfect? No, but I can trust that He will help me learn from everything we've experienced, even be proud of what I've done well, and deal with my responsibilities with Him by my side. In His grace, I can be the mom my son needs. Regardless of the past, the future remains to be written. Trust God to help you finish what you've started, in the safety of His grace.

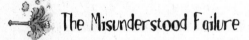 ## The Misunderstood Failure

Sometimes, when things are going badly and we've experienced a lot of failures, we begin to see everything as a failure. A job we don't get is a failure. A relationship that doesn't work out is a failure. A deal that fell through is a failure. But maybe we're not seeing things clearly. Maybe we're looking for one kind of success and God is looking for another. We must be willing to trust that God's view is a little clearer than ours.

Here's a quick example: Out of my own need one day, I invented a tool to help crafters and others who sew or iron, and I decided that it would make a fortune. (I know, crazy, huh?) Imagine my disappointment when that never happened. After awhile, I boxed my failures up carefully and added their worthlessness to my ever-growing list.

Then one day, many months later, the director of a nonprofit group that makes blankets for sick children discovered my little tool from an obscure Web page that I had forgotten was even online. Did I have any available? she wanted to know. Hmm, let's see. . .how many would she like?

God had seen to it that I *did* have some available, all safe and secure, just waiting to go where they were needed. So how can I call my only venture into invention a failure? By my original standards, it certainly was; but God had found a better plan than mine, and that is just one example. If He can take my small effort and find a way to use it, how can I not trust Him to take *all* of my efforts and somehow, someday, grace me with the understanding of their purpose? What I don't understand *right now* may just be more wonders in the making.

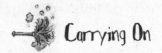 ## Carrying On

All of those types of failures are a part of our lives, and even the strongest among us can feel burdened by them. We want to trust in God, and we want to change our lives; but the failures make us weak and afraid. No matter what kind of failure we're struggling with, we usually have a strangling dose of doubt to accompany it—doubt that we can ever do anything right, doubt that God could really accept and forgive our mess, doubt that we have anything left to contribute even if God somehow decided He was willing to help us in our building. No wonder our frames are about to break!

Doubt is heavy and relentless, the direct enemy of trust. Give doubt the chance, and it'll start a fight every time. One of its weapons is the unimportant view of everyone else that it beats you over the head with. Doubt points out that others carry on and pile victory atop victory while we stand still, afraid to try anything, fearing piles of dust atop dust. But trust in the Lord is a scrappy fighter, and it won't let you stand still. The Lord understands our doubt and everything that comes with it. He who has never failed somehow knows just what it feels like for us. So He waits for that heartbeat that lets Him in, so that He can knock the doubt out of your life and replace it with grace.

Trusting God to help you carry on even when you doubt isn't about your failure or success as you see it or as anyone else sees it. It's all about the change in your mind and your heart. "But let each one examine his own work, and then he will have rejoicing in himself alone, and not in another. For each one shall bear his own load" (Galatians 6:4–5 NKJV).

Get personal with God about the failures that hurt so. He can show you how to use them all, and even the doubt, too, because He will waste nothing in your life. Just because you've not lived out your dreams and plans *so far* doesn't mean that you are destined to live a life abandoned and incomplete. You are valuable to Him, and He'll give you all of the grace you need to respond to the load you carry.

> *Oh, taste and see that the LORD is good;*
> *blessed is the man who trusts in Him!*
>
> PSALM 34:8 NKJV

Applying God's grace to your life is not checking it off a list of behaviors you hope to cultivate. It's not covering an injured spot with ointment and a bandage. It is infusing the most gracious of gifts into your spirit while you and God build a resting place together, a place where you can find solace in His peace and inspiration for your work.

Then the wonderful and amazing experiences of a grace-filled life begin, all because you were willing to trust instead of doubt. When you fail, you learn from your pain. When you resolve to carry on, you learn from God. Don't you know He just loves the lessons on those days?!

We are hard pressed on every side,
but not crushed;
perplexed, but not in despair; persecuted,
but not abandoned;
struck down, but not destroyed.

2 CORINTHIANS 4:8–9 NIV

As long as we are "not destroyed," the lessons aren't over. The grace isn't spent. The change in us can continue. We can delight with the Lord in our transformation from beginning to end, from the depth of our distance away from Him when we allow it to the heights of our companionship with Him when we trust in His grace.

There is no failure that can put us so far from Him that we can't learn something else about His capacity for grace. Even the big failures—the failed relationships or failed beliefs, the failure to worship or the failure to repent—are not too big for God's broom. Our frames can't begin to hold them all in, but our God can't wait to get at them. The path is through us, through the trust that inches us the tiniest way toward the redemption we must believe in before it can touch us.

Command those who are rich in this
present age not to be haughty,
nor to trust in uncertain riches
but in the living God,
who gives us richly all things to enjoy.

1 TIMOTHY 6:17 NKJV

Nothing you ever accomplish will touch you until it's been touched by God, because "unless the LORD builds the house, they labor in vain who build it" (Psalm 127:1 NKJV). Unless you apply God's grace to your failures, they are mightier than you are.

The Blessings of Success

Sometimes we can get so tied up in looking at our failures that we fail to inspect our successes. Have you ever discounted the successes you did enjoy because of the ten-year-old failure that you still carry around like today's newspaper? I have. Sometimes that's because we judge too harshly any victory that we achieve, finding fault with the parts that aren't perfect. It's more likely we'll point out the flaws even if they're tiny because we're so much more comfortable with that approach. We translate never perfect into never satisfying.

God's grace says no! There is wonderful joy in even the smallest success. Anything that isn't a failure is a success. Anywhere that we apply a lesson learned is a testament of our faith in God and ourselves. Anytime that we make progress is a time that we're changing, and that's the Lord's goal. All of our success is cause for celebration.

Whoever gives heed to instruction prospers,
and blessed is he who trusts in the LORD.

PROVERBS 16:20 NIV

He teaches; we learn. He reaches; we respond. He sees everything; we understand as far as our trust allows. Our frame becomes stronger with His patches of grace. Our future becomes surer with our letting go of the past. Our transformation becomes real with dust we've traded for peace, failures we've traded for trust.

That miracle of a change only happens when we listen to what our Father has to say, when we trust what we hear and submit our failures to His grace. That kind of change, in even incremental ways, is always a blessed success.

* * * * *

 Sweeping Away the Dust. . .

- How have you let your failures separate you from God's grace? How much time have you spent complaining about what isn't fair?
- Can you view your failures differently when you see them in God's "transformational tool kit"?

- What can you learn from your finished failures, your unfinished failures, and your misunderstood failures—and how can you apply God's grace to them?
- How will you carry on when the doubts threaten to overpower you? What blessings has the Lord given to you when you've trusted Him instead?

* * * * *

Lord, by Your grace, I can deal with the failures of my life and continue to build a dwelling place for You. Please help me trust in Your ability to use all that I am and all that I have. Amen.

Chapter 7

Transforming Sorrow into Hope

*He heals the brokenhearted
and binds up their wounds.*

PSALM 147:3 NIV

Sometimes our imperfections surface in our failures, and our journey toward grace starts there. Never content with just one problem, though, we have no trouble focusing on the aching sorrow that also breaks our hearts; and if we're not careful, we'll let that sorrow distance us from the Lord, too. We'll let a broken and battered frame crumble in pieces while we give up on God.

Even if we still hold fast to the trust we've built, we hurt too much to feel the hope God offers. And without it, we are a withering vine in the desert. But God's hope is never far away.

I know how it feels, that hurt in your heart that goes all the way through to your soul and back again. The pain is tangible and real, a true ache that you can feel in your body that comes from the sorrow of abandonment or disappointment. The more we hurt, the more we cower, figuratively (and sometimes literally) all balled up in a fetal position just waiting for the next blow. We can't see beyond the tears in our eyes, and our heart clamps down fast as a mousetrap, capturing all the ugly hurt and holding on tight.

The sorrow can come from anywhere—from our own actions, from dreams unfulfilled, from the persecution of others. Whatever the cause, the effect is the same—a loss of hope in ourselves, our future, our Lord. But that hope we need is far more than it appears to be on the surface. It's much more than a blind wish for things to get better. It's a sustaining anticipation of the Lord's blessings, based on a trust that says He loves us enough to give them to us. And once we feel the hope, we can move on to the purpose, to His work. Hope allows us to carry on, to think toward the future, to break the hold that our imperfections have on us.

Misplaced Hope

When we lose hope, all we can see is what's gone wrong and what's unsatisfying or disappointing in our lives. It is then that the grace of God seems like the fleeting scenes of a dream when you awake, out of your grasp and unlikely to return. The sorrow wins, and God cries right along with you.

The interpretation we have that gets us into this hopeless place is that narrow and shortsighted one again, the one that puts more stock in our lack of perfection and the status of our flaws than our bounty of opportunity and the status of our hearts.

We stack up a giant dust pile (and justify it because the aches and pains of our soul are so very real), and then we give it a permanent address, as if we will never be touched by God's merciful hand, as if we are destined to live in the quagmire of sorrow that, somehow, we must deserve. What a mess!

Sometimes, in this state, we turn to even more destructive means to deal with it. Addictions of all kinds can prevail when we lose hope, and the worst may be an addiction to trying to solve our problems ourselves. When we create elaborate ways to overcome the sorrow, everything from escaping through drugs to denying our dreams, we still don't find the hope we need. We only get another kick in the teeth and another rip in our frame because our methods begin with a trust misplaced in some hopeless addiction that is even weaker and more limited than we are.

The Lord watches our ineffective human attempts to reconcile the pain just like we do, knowing the outcome before we even start. But while we bring only sad discouragement and imperfect understanding to the sorrow of our hearts, the Lord offers His unique treatment that hinges only on one perfect breath that dares to hope.

His pleasure is not in the strength of the horse,
nor his delight in the legs of a man;
the Lord delights in those who fear
him, who put their hope in his unfailing love.

PSALM 147:10–11 NIV

Anything that makes us look for hope in a place other than God's grace will fail. Anything that says it's more powerful than God will fail. Anything that replaces the sorrow with more of the same will fail. We need hope to overcome the dust that sorrow brings, and hope in God is the only kind that will work.

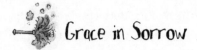 Grace in Sorrow

God's grace is so multifaceted—it redeems us and comforts us. It is the powerful, undeniable side of God and also the compassionate, restorative side of God. It is in the failure and the sorrow that we seek "to grasp how wide and long and high and deep is the love of Christ" (Ephesians 3:18 NIV).

Understanding the love of Christ is hard for us imperfect humans to do! We sometimes try to force it into a definition of the love that we understand in our limited human ways. We feel His love in a moment here or there, and then we remember how unworthy we are. We do something else wrong or showcase a particularly disturbing imperfection, and there we are again—outside the reach of that perfect love. Or the circumstances in our lives are so horrible that we can't even begin to look for that love again, justifying to ourselves why we must carry this burden alone. When the sorrow of a broken heart is so raw and so big, it's hard to believe that there could ever be enough love and grace to reach us.

But the love of Christ is unique. It's always wide and long and high and deep enough for any burden simply because it's *God's will*. He knew the aches and pains we would feel, so He made His love and His grace wide and long and high and deep enough to carry us through them. Before the sorrow overcame us, He understood us. And He knows the process we must go through to get back to Him.

 Losing Hope

Losing hope is easy because it's so easy to become discouraged by the sorrow of our world. We find ourselves in tears all the time when the hurt overtakes everything, and there is no hope because we can't see beyond right now that's already a mess. Why hope in a future that we're likely to damage as well?

Save me, O God!
For the waters have come up to my neck.
I sink in deep mire, where there is no standing;
I have come into
deep waters, where the floods overflow me.
I am weary with my crying;
my throat is dry;
my eyes fail while I wait for my God.

PSALM 69:1–3 NKJV

Oh, I know that "waters up to my neck" feeling! I can remember times when I felt about as useful as "boots on a horse" as my dad says. You probably know that feeling, too. It hits when your professional life is nowhere near where you want it to be, or when your personal relationships are shot, or just when you feel that you have no more to contribute to this world than a body you could donate to science.

Sometimes, I've felt that my frame was about to collapse completely. I've felt the dust piling higher and higher as I struggled, and then I've just given in to the pain. I've given in to the hopelessness and wasted time wallowing in the sorrowful state of nothingness, never once thinking about going to God for some grace to get me through.

Losing hope is always our next logical (human) step when times are tough.

When the sorrow wins, we lose all hope and feel no strength to get it back. I've felt the physical drain that comes from losing hope; and worse, I've lived the emotional drain that makes you think that there will never be a happy day in your life again. When I would think of God and His thoughts on my mess, I would imagine Him somewhere shaking His head, as sorrowful as I was about His daughter who became one big pile of dust. Could it be that He would grant me one more small serving of grace? Was there still hope somewhere?

Dare I cry louder and ask for some help? "Be merciful to me, O LORD, for I am in distress; my eyes grow weak with sorrow, my soul and my body with grief" (Psalm 31:9 NIV). Would He answer me?

It's in that dull pit of your soul and body, where your heart feels abandoned by God and when your weakness is stronger than your will to overcome, that your imperfections seem like giant mountains in your way. But God sees them as they really are, only dust; and He's never bothered by that. The tears we cry are of more concern to Him—they focus us on the dust; they focus Him on *us*.

 Seeking Hope

Finally, when you can't cry anymore and you can't slash another rip in your frame, you'll feel that "spent" feeling that says you can't go on like this anymore. That hurts, but it's a turning point. You have to make a choice—you have to be ready to change, one way or the other. God's waiting on your answer.

You can accept the sorrow that's eating your heart by the second and take your chances at handling it yourself, or you can seek the grace of God that can heal any hurt, even one that belongs to imperfect and resistant and unworthy you. The question is the same: Are you ready to change?

He wants to take your sorrow and give you hope in its place. He wants you to stop trying to heal yourself and believe instead in His gracious power to do it so much better.

Hear me, O Lord,
for Your lovingkindness is good;
turn to me according to the multitude
of Your tender mercies. . . .
But I am poor and sorrowful;
let Your salvation,
O God, set me up on high.

PSALM 69:16, 29 NKJV

With the choice to pursue the change God wants in your life, you open up your broken heart to the hope that will jump-start it like a jolt of power to a dead battery. Try it your way, alone, and see if it works, if you must. But while that method buries you deeper in the dust of a sorrow you can't possibly explain, God's method brings you out of the dust and into the comfort of His power. "Seek hope in Me," He says, "and that will be enough."

The Lord's grace presents itself to you in whatever way you need. When your hurt is a flame on a wildfire, His grace is the ice pack to your burning heart. His "tender mercies" know how raw you feel deep inside, how vulnerable you feel outside, and He will "set you on high," protect and heal you from the effects of the sorrow and dissatisfaction in your life. He knows how much damage a loss of hope can do to you, and He'll help you overcome those feelings if you'll grasp for the hope that comes gift wrapped in His grace.

Choosing to seek God's grace alone moves the sorrow out of the way so that the Lord can get to work on the cracks in your frame. You can't be a part of that work without a hope in Him and the future He has planned for you—a future that won't be tied to the sorrow in your heart but instead to the strength in your spirit. And that's a strength that can only be supported by something stronger, by God and His unlimited grace.

The Lord's grace is not just a remedy for the pain you're feeling right now, but a prescription for a lifetime bound to be hit with sorrow again. His grace will always return you to a place of hope so that you can go on to more wonderful blessings, buoyed by His love and encouraged by His touch. "A cheerful heart is good medicine, but a crushed spirit dries up the bones" (Proverbs 17:22 NIV).

Finding Hope

The second you turn your spirit away from the dust piles of sorrow and aches and tears—*that very second*—you give your heart and mind permission to believe again. And you can't find the hope God supplies until you believe it exists. You haven't forgotten about God's love or even doubted its power—you've just misplaced your belief in your sorrow.

The loss is not permanent, though, and the Lord's grace prevails. He is there, just waiting for the tiniest opening, the tiniest invitation, and He reminds us generously of His tender power.

Because of the LORD's great love
we are not consumed,
for his compassions never fail.
They are new every morning;
great is your faithfulness.

LAMENTATIONS 3:22–23 NIV

Believing in the Lord's faithfulness lets us draw a peaceful breath for a moment, and that's all He needs. When we rest in His hope, we have to be close to Him. When we're close to Him, we can talk to Him, listen to Him, and allow ourselves to receive all of the blessings He's been holding just for us.

The Lord restores the hope we've lost in so many ways. Our discovery is never boring! He may send a friend when we need encouragement. We may experience a victory. He may speak to us in a new way, getting our attention and instilling a new sense of excitement and purpose in our lives. Everything hinges on our belief in a hope we can't yet see.

But as for me, I watch in hope for the LORD,
I wait for God my Savior; my God will hear me.
Do not gloat over me, my enemy!
Though I have fallen, I will rise.
Though I sit in darkness,
the LORD will be my light.

MICAH 7:7–8 NIV

When we believe that the sorrow can't last forever, that there has to be an end to the hurt, then we can look for ways God makes that real to us. When we believe that He will extend His grace to us and help us find hope again, then we can recognize it when it arrives. When we believe that we can stretch over the dust with God, then we will feel the hope that guides the first step—a hope in a Lord who loves us enough to hear and answer our cries.

The righteous cry out,
and the LORD hears them;
he delivers them from all their troubles.
The LORD is close to the brokenhearted and
saves those who are crushed in spirit.

PSALM 34:17–18 NIV

When the Lord comes near to your broken heart and crushed spirit, He restores hope to your wandering soul. You can go from seeking hope to experiencing hope. Both the journey and the destination are a partnership with God that you don't want to miss. His transforming grace allows you to leave the sorrow behind so that you can build on the hope that lies ahead.

 Revealing Hope

Finding the hope that you need to go on means reconnecting with your Lord, feeling His compassion, trusting in His power, and seeking the only rescue that will ever save you from the sorrow of your heart. When you make that choice, when you want to change the sorrow into hope, you will feel the effects.

> *Now may the God of hope fill you with*
> *all joy and peace in believing,*
> *that you may abound in hope by the*
> *power of the Holy Spirit.*

ROMANS 15:13 NKJV

With joy and peace filling you, there is no worry about a weak frame. There is only the application of grace to your sorrowful heart so that your redeemed and powerful heart can sustain anything this world throws at it. The hope you feel in getting closer to God is the hope you carry into the world, and it's all you need.

And then the change you promised God is

all you can think about! The pain and heartache give way to hope and faith. But it's not an "I'll think about it tomorrow" kind of pushing the sorrow aside. It doesn't mean that you won't still hurt, because healing takes time.

The transformation within you does mean that you will see beyond the hurt to a God who will guide you wherever you need to go, and you'll trust Him to be there with you now and forever. It means that you can allow a little hope into a world that has seemed hopeless. It means that you'll feel the courage and enthusiasm to go on, to try again, to look for something positive amid the pain, for miracles amid the misery.

I pray also that the eyes of your heart
may be enlightened in order
that you may know the hope
to which he has called you,
the riches of his glorious inheritance in the saints,
and his incomparably great power
for us who believe.
That power is like the working
of his mighty strength.

EPHESIANS 1:18–19 NIV

God's hope comes to us in the saddest of times. It's part of what we need to do our work because it helps us face the dust we can't keep out of our world. When we choose to let God transform our sorrow into hope, everything changes. We go from stalled to active, from spent to charged. We won't see a life of instant perfection, but we'll feel a life of unlimited possibility. The Lord's grace makes anything possible; and with that kind of hope, the sorrow cannot last.

That relief is guaranteed from the Lord who since time began "loved us and by his grace gave us eternal encouragement and good hope" (2 Thessalonians 2:16 NIV). And with that hope, you are free to focus on your purpose here, wrapped in God's amazing grace.

* * * * *

Sweeping Away the Dust...

- What are the sorrows you're holding on to that are drowning your hope?

- How have you tried unsuccessfully to deal with your hopelessness in the past? Why did you make those choices?
- When the waters are "up to your neck," how do you respond? Do you try to rescue yourself or turn to God?
- How can you apply your hope in God and His grace to your life and sorrows right now?

* * * * *

Lord, by Your grace, *I can overcome my sorrows and find hope in Your love and compassion. Please help me through and past my hurt to the life of joy and service You have planned for me. Amen.*

Chapter 8

Transforming Regret into Purpose

If you, O LORD, kept a record of sins,
O Lord, who could stand?

PSALM 130:3 NIV

We perfectionists are masters at regret, aren't we? We can spend years in regret over something that others wouldn't even remember. And when we have a really big "something" to honestly regret, well, everyone might as well just get out of the way and let us wallow in it, because listening to any kind of reasoning isn't something we're likely to do.

And while we're wallowing in our regret and wondering if there is anything worse we could do (no matter what it is we've done), we convince ourselves that the Lord is disgusted with us, too.

But what is He doing instead? He's over there, in the same place we left Him, scratching His head and wondering why we've missed the point—again.

He's not keeping a record of everything we've done wrong. Instead, He's continually offering us a chance to do something right, forever adjusting our path to reach the goals He's planned for us. And what has come before is no match for what He sees in the future. Our job is to leave the regret behind, to learn and move on.

But it's hard.

 Dwelling On the Past

Experience may be the best teacher, but it's sometimes a cruel one. We have to live and learn, and sometimes we do make terrible mistakes. What is it that makes us do some of the things we do? And why, even when we know better, do we still get involved in things that will only hurt us?

Poor judgment may be one answer. Confusion is another. And there are a million more, but the bottom line is a trust and hope in something besides God. We move away from Him; we make a mistake; we pay the price. And we often inflict the heaviest cost on ourselves. Our regret becomes an anchor around our necks and a wall between us and God. There is a better way, and guess what? He's there to help you!

And God is able to make all grace abound to you,
so that in all things at all times,
having all that you need,
you will abound in every good work.

2 CORINTHIANS 9:8 NIV

There is *purpose* to that truth! You will "abound in every good work." Do you see that? If your heart is weighed down with regret and resistant to moving forward because of what you've done in the past, you're wasting one of God's greatest blessings.

Don't you think that included in "all that you need" is the ability to deal with your mistakes and make some use out of them? Of course there is. God won't waste one second of your life, even if you feel that you have. He won't see the broken woman you think you are; instead, He will see the disciple who can meet her life's purpose, even if she has a few things to overcome.

If you're dealing with a substance abuse problem, an affair, a criminal record, an estranged relationship with a family member, or any number of other bad situations, you have a lot to handle, no question about it. But your life *remains*. Your work *remains*. Your God *remains* to sweep away everything in your way, patch the most painful cracks in your frame, and support you in your work. He's not going to give up on you. And if you give up, you're letting both of you down.

> *Do you not know? Have you not heard?*
> *The LORD is the everlasting God, the*
> *Creator of the ends of the earth.*
> *He will not grow tired or weary, and*
> *his understanding no one can fathom.*
> *He gives strength to the weary and*
> *increases the power of the weak.*
>
> ISAIAH 40:28–29 NIV

Regret drags you down in a way unmatched by other emotions. When you feel the full brunt of your sins, you want to bury yourself in your dust pile, figuring that whatever bad things happen to you are deserved.

When your mind and heart are attacked by regret, you create this little imaginary box. Inside that box, you lock away the good things you've done (probably no more than two or three things in your whole life); then you shove that box out into the ocean, and the ocean represents all of the bad things you've done.

You let the bad swallow up and destroy the good! Big mistakes are tough to deal with, but they don't have to be all that you are. Certainly, they are a part of you, but what you become because of or in spite of them is up to you and God. He is far stronger than anything you've done wrong.

Great is our Lord, and mighty in power;
His understanding is infinite.

PSALM 147:5 NKJV

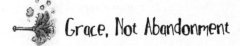 Grace, Not Abandonment

It's God's grace that allows us to live with our mistakes. Left to our own interpretation, we would exile ourselves to the deepest regions of the world's most treacherous pit and set up housekeeping there.

Once you were alienated from God
and were enemies in your minds
because of your evil behavior.
But now he has reconciled you by
Christ's physical body through death to
present you holy in his sight,
without blemish and free from accusation.

COLOSSIANS 1:21–22 NIV

We let our regrets convince us sometimes that we are destined for a worthless life, that nothing positive or redeeming remains in us because of our mistakes. We abandon our future to the past; so it stands to reason, in our minds, that God has abandoned us, too. But His grace doesn't withdraw from us when we're afraid and alone. That's the exact time He reaches for *us*.

The Lord will help you out of the past and into the here and now where He needs you if you'll respond to His grace. He can't see you live out your purpose if He abandons you. And He has put far too much work in you already not to keep loving you through your mistakes. If He abandons you, He is being untrue. And we both know that that can never be.

Acceptance, Not Justification

You don't have to justify your past to accept it.
You don't have to excuse whatever you've done to
deal with it. Maybe you were in a bad place
when you slipped. Maybe you talked yourself
into believing that your choices wouldn't hurt
others. Maybe you rationalized everything
because of the pain you were in at the time. Or
maybe you were just unthinking and irresponsi-
ble. The point is—it doesn't matter.

The facts remain the same. You can't take
back anything you've done or said. You can't
rewrite the story and make different choices. But
with God's grace, you can do so much more.

*Forgetting what is behind and straining
toward what is ahead,
I press on toward the goal to win
the prize for which
God called me heavenward in Christ Jesus.*

PHILIPPIANS 3:13–14 NIV

You can realize that the Lord is still there waiting for you. He's still got an agenda. He's still got a plan. The question is, what are you going to do about your part of it?

Learning from our past is an important part of our journey with God. And learning doesn't involve finding excuses. Nowhere does God say that you must have had a good reason for everything you've done. Nowhere does He say that a good reason would mitigate your regret. Nowhere does He say that if you excuse your behavior, it'll teach you anything.

Instead, He tells you to keep working, to "press on," to leave the past behind and concentrate on the future. You must trade your regrets of the past for God's preoccupation with the future. There is *purpose* there. Accept what has come before and prepare for what remains.

 Understanding, Not Arrogance

God's grace helps you accept your past, and then He sticks around to teach you how to overcome all of those imperfect thoughts you're having about what to do next. Sometimes we think that if He's been kind enough to forgive us our sins, we'll know how to not commit any more because we've certainly learned our lesson this time!

We probably do learn some lessons after one horrific encounter, but it usually takes more instruction. With the attitude that we've learned all we need to know, we'll miss out on a beautiful part of our relationship with the Lord, the compassionate unfolding of His grace in new circumstances. We need to understand how God's grace continues, how it is a steady flow *through* us, not just a brief dousing *over* us.

Therefore, rid yourselves of all malice
and all deceit, hypocrisy, envy, and
slander of every kind. Like newborn babies,
crave pure spiritual milk,
so that by it you may grow up in your salvation,
now that you have
tasted that the Lord is good.

1 PETER 2:1–3 NIV

Become like babies, the Lord tells us. Our journey truly begins when we start over, knowing nothing and needing everything. That's okay.

If the regret is so painful that it pushes us to an embarrassing feeling of weakness and loss, we don't have to try to hide it and pretend we can handle it on our own. Babies need lots of help. Sometimes, so do we.

God's grace will carry us through every step and mile of the journey to the purpose He has in mind for us. If we have to start like a baby learning to crawl, He'll start there. Your transformation begins wherever you are.

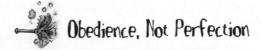 Obedience, Not Perfection

Once we accept our past and understand how to begin our transformation, we often start to worry about our pace and our performance. Not necessary.

As obedient children, do not conform
to the evil desires you had
when you lived in ignorance.
But just as he who called you is holy,
so be holy in all you do.

1 PETER 1:14–15 NIV

That does *not* mean that we have to be perfect! The Lord still knows what a feeble frame we're working with here. He desires our obedience, but He also desires our companionship. "Be holy in all you do" is the command. "Be like Me, trust in Me, hope in Me, come with Me on this wonderful journey that is your life," God says.

He doesn't say, "Be perfect, or I won't love you." He doesn't say, "Meet this deadline, or the deal's off." Again, He addresses us as children, as those needing instruction and guidance, as those growing in their faith, walking with the best Teacher in the world.

> *You are my portion, O LORD;*
> *I have promised to obey your words.*
> *I have sought your face with all my heart;*
> *be gracious to me according to your promise.*
> *I have considered my ways and have turned*
> *my steps to your statutes.*
> *I will hasten and not delay to*
> *obey your commands.*
>
> PSALM 119:57–60 NIV

That "portion" is our greatest possession—a personal relationship with our God, who will be there to guide our steps and chart our path. Regardless of our "ways" in the past, our future is what we make it. We can turn our steps at any time.

Imperfect, we can obey the Lord's commands. Perfect, He will save us with His grace and steer us with His instruction. His perfection will always override any imperfect strides we make. Our job is to keep going.

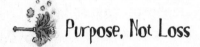

Purpose, Not Loss

We have to deal with the dust while we do our work. We have to accept the past and make the decision to transform the future. We have to try to see our lives the way God sees them. And He sees them as valuable. Anything less discounts His judgment.

Failure can direct us, even if it's embarrassing. Whatever we have suffered can strengthen us, even if it hurts. Whatever we have done can teach us, even if it's not pretty. No matter what, our imperfection cannot separate us from the Lord. The life we may see as lost or worthless is still here on a mission, divinely guided and full of purpose.

And whatever you do in word or deed,
do all in the name of the Lord Jesus,
giving thanks to God the Father
through Him.

COLOSSIANS 3:17 NKJV

There is no loss in our feeble frames; there is only purpose, because we can't lose God. And as long as He is still with us, still supporting us, still sweeping our dust away, we can carry on. He still has a plan.

We cannot be misdirected or misguided when we follow the Lord's lead. Every regret that we have is something He can use for a purpose. Finding that purpose is part of the great journey in His grace, and you know the path by now: We have to be close to Him to know our purpose, and we have to accept His grace to be close to Him, and we have to ask for His grace to accept it.

One small choice leads us to the great possibilities and experiences that He has designed for us. He won't reveal those to us unless we're listening, but He won't give them to somebody else, either. Your purpose, like your past, is unique.

Feeling the regret of a lifetime of imperfection can make you feel that all is lost, that there is nothing left in you to give. But no, the Lord has put in us more wonder than we'll discover in a dozen lifetimes! We can only hope to have our eyes opened to the blessings that we can see in eighty or one hundred years! There is no room for obsession with your regret when your God-given purpose is your focus. How can we call anything loss when it all leads to Him?

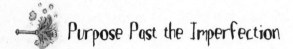

Purpose Past the Imperfection

I've never met anyone who didn't have some regrets. And I have my share. If you don't have any yet, you probably will. It's part of our imperfect nature, try as we might to deny it.

And with every regret comes pain. None of us likes to make mistakes! None of us is proud of failing God, our family, or ourselves. It hurts when we see how we've damaged our life or the lives of others. But in all of the regret, the Lord never loses us. He never gives up hope for us. He never forgets why He gave us this life to live, "for it is God who works in you to will and to act according to his good purpose" (Philippians 2:13 NIV).

If He is still working in you, then you can get past the regret and find your purpose. Because to say that the Lord "wants to work in you but can't quite manage it" is ridiculous. Do you want to question His ability, His determination? I didn't think so.

You, in all of your imperfection, can live and love and accomplish in this imperfect world *according to His good purpose* because the Lord wants you to. It's that simple. Despite everything else in your life, everything that is past and yet to come, God can nurse you through the pain and guide you on to your purpose.

But He won't force you. Remember that it is we who must make that decision to submit the dust of our lives to the grace of God. It is we who must seek the only true relief from our pain. It is our choice that the Lord is waiting for.

So, do you want to transform your regret into purpose? Take a breath of trust, expose your faulty frame to the Lord, and grant Him access to your dust. He'll wrap you in His grace in return. Pretty good trade, huh? Then the amazing blessings of His purpose will begin to work in you. You'll have no time for regret because you'll be far too busy walking with the

Lord on a journey uniquely yours in a life
abundantly blessed.

* * * * *

 Sweeping Away the Dust. . .

- What are your biggest regrets? How have
  you let them tether you to a past you cannot change?
- How have you misunderstood God's grace
  in the past and viewed it as a finite gift
  instead of an ongoing application? How
  have you tried to escape your regrets instead
  of learn from them?
- How can you obey God and still come to
  terms with your imperfection? How will His
  grace guide you on your journey to discover
  your purpose?
- If there were no regrets in your life, how
  would you see your life's purpose? How
  have you let your regrets change your view?

* * * * *

Lord, by Your grace, *I can dismiss my regrets and focus instead on the work that awaits. Please help me take this damaged life and find its purpose. Amen.*

Part 3

"Hey, Wanna See My Grout?!"

The *Appreciation* of God's Grace

*"For it will not be you speaking,
but the Spirit of your Father
speaking through you."*

MATTHEW 10:20 NIV

"I can feel the grout in this rickety ole frame now, Lord. It feels safe and thick and strong, even though I still feel fragile on the inside now and then; but I love this grout! I want to focus on it and protect it and strengthen it. But how?"

"Expose it."

"Excuse me? I know I said I love it, but it's not all that attractive. It's strong evidence of some pretty strong dust, You know."

"No, it's irrefutable evidence of the strongest love in the world. Mine. Understand?"

"I think I do."

* * * * *

Chapter 9

We're All Dust

And we, who with unveiled
faces all reflect the Lord's glory,
are being transformed into his
likeness with ever-increasing glory,
which comes from the Lord,
who is the Spirit.

2 CORINTHIANS 3:18 NIV

One of the greatest by-products of God's grace is the view it gives us of the rest of the world, the view that says "we're not so different after all." And that comforts us. We want to know that there's nothing terribly "abnormal" about us, that we're actually not the exception to the rule of God's grace after all.

And that's what we learn, in His beautiful and perfectly delivered way, that there isn't now and can never be an exception to the rule of His grace. There is nothing abnormal about our failures and imperfections. There is nothing different about the way He will deal with them. There is nothing so remarkable or scary about our dust that could cause it to repel the Lord's broom.

I can remember experiencing this "revelation" more than once (being one of God's daughters who requires remedial work); and the feeling is both relief and empathy, resting in the clean spot the Lord has made. That revelation is the beginning of a wonderful part of God's grace, the part that allows us to see that all of us "throughout the world are undergoing the same kind of sufferings" (1 Peter 5:9 NIV). That reflection says we're all the same.

Never Alone, Never Different

We don't want to be alone, and yet we hide our dust because we're afraid that we already are. God's grace proves us wrong. He enlightens us with the amazing realization that it's not our dust that is so special—it's His grace. Your past is different from mine, but our need is the same. His work with you is different from His work with me, but the goal is the same.

God didn't play favorites when He created us. He didn't give some of us a charmed life and some of us a doomed life. Regardless of what we see outwardly of others' lives, we can rest assured that each one of us is sitting in the same classroom, trying to learn from our mistakes, appreciate the Lord's grace, and understand His will for our lives.

The dust that spills from the cracks in your frame requires God's unique touch for your unique hurt; and once you experience that healing, you understand that my frame is cracked, too! It's not a smug, "so you're not perfect, either" jab at me, but a response of awe in a God who can deal with anything. Once you experience the Lord's grace, you see instantly the wonders He has done for me and others. You see that what remains for Him to do for you and me is unlimited and cannot be sidelined by a little dust.

You see that He's already factored in all of your imperfections and that everything you feared before is nothing. His grace supply never diminishes. Every worry about being too imperfect for His work disintegrates like the bright sparks from fireworks in the sky—they make a lot of noise but amount to nothing.

Your need for His grace is no greater or smaller than mine, because it's all the same to Him. We're all dust—arranged differently perhaps, but still His needy daughters who have more in common than we think. And that's a big blessing.

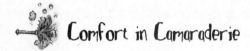 ## Comfort in Camaraderie

Feeling alone in any situation is scary, and feeling alienated because of our imperfections is a terrible ache for our hearts. But as we learn to apply God's saving grace to our failures and sorrows and regrets, we learn, sometimes by surprise, that others have traveled this same road before, "for there is no difference between Jew and Gentile—the same Lord is Lord of all and richly blesses all who call on him" (Romans 10:12 NIV).

When we are able to look out without fear into the world again, we see those same people we thought were so different; and, suddenly, we see that they aren't more or less perfect or more or less deserving than we are. We see that the dust of these earthly lives isn't picky—it attaches itself to everyone, no matter what, and can only be dislodged one way.

Knowing that the ground is leveled brings us a great sense of relief because then we feel the comfort of those who feel the way we do. We realize that our irrational fears were the same ones that others have felt or are feeling now. Understanding that single point brings us a great sense of responsibility, as well.

> *Do your best to present yourself to*
> *God as one approved,*
> *a workman who does not*
> *need to be ashamed*
> *and who correctly handles the*
> *word of truth.*
>
> 2 TIMOTHY 2:15 NIV

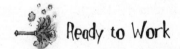 Ready to Work

I'll bet that you won't ever meet one person who's experienced God's grace so much that she sees no need for further interaction with Him.

That's a silly bet, isn't it? So the flip side must be that none of us could ever experience enough of God's grace. None of us—regardless of what you see of anyone else's life—can ever establish ourselves outside the need for God's grace.

Everyone you meet is struggling with some imperfection. And everyone you meet (and I hope it's me one day!) can benefit from the encouragement of *your* experience. Once you have tasted the bitter of this world and the sweet of God's grace, your eyes are opened. You're able to see how your sisters, like me, need to be nourished by that same love the Lord has shared with you. Please, don't hold back! He's given you all you need to understand my quest and to help me understand Him through yours—His grace personified in *you*.

When you've walked hand in hand with God on your journey of grace, your heart is never the same; and in its transformed state, you can "rejoice with those who rejoice, and weep with those who weep" (Romans 12:15 NKJV). And isn't that an amazing part of the job you've been called to do!

In holding God's hand, we realize that everyone is just like we are on the inside, even when the outside looks a lot different. Everyone else is imperfect, unworthy, and loved, just like we are.

In that shared condition, we develop valuable tools that make us valuable workers for the Lord.

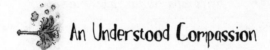

An Understood Compassion

We are unmercifully hard on ourselves when we're struggling with our dust. We can't stand to even look at it! But through His love and kindness, God is merciful beyond measure; and His view of our dust makes us strong and mended, able to go out into the world with a warm sense of belonging that we've never known before.

And while we're amazed at the depth of God's love and grace, we see, finally, what He sees. He knew before the beginning that we would all be dusty shells dependent on Him. And He knew that our shared imperfection would be a link that would work to His glory and purpose.

When we understand this connection, we *want* to reach out to those we see suffering, in need and alone. Like a secret too delicious to keep, we want to lead our sisters toward this same gift, toward this same satisfaction in seeking their life's purpose. The Lord tells us how.

Finally, all of you, live in harmony
with one another;
be sympathetic, love as brothers,
be compassionate and humble.

1 PETER 3:8 NIV

Walking your own path from afraid and ashamed to forgiven and redeemed puts everything and everyone you see in a different light, in a God-corralled light that makes you unable to hold such glories and blessings in.

When we understand that there are others out there hurting just like we've hurt, fighting their own imperfections and disappointments, God's grace in us comes out through a compassion unlike any other. We don't have to know the exact cause and feelings of another's pain, but we know the need it creates. You know where I am when I say, "It hurts."

Any embarrassment or shame we've felt from our past is transformed into an empathy and understanding for those just like us. The cracks we tried so hard to hide are now patched testament to a merciful God's incalculable grace; and from that cradle of His love, we are renewed, transformed, and thankful for the gift we've been given. And that gift creates in us a compassion reflective of God's own.

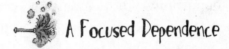

A Focused Dependence

Along with God's grace, we get a glimpse into His unbelievable power. We see how He can take the biggest mess we can make and transform it somehow into an instrument for His purpose. We see that power, but we can't really understand it in the constraints of our human minds. That's okay—the mystery of the Lord's unending love makes it no less real. And we don't have to explain it to appreciate it.

Lord, my heart is not haughty, nor my eyes lofty.
Neither do I concern myself with great matters,
nor with things too profound for me.

PSALM 131:1 NKJV

We are eternally thankful for God's grace and amazed by its power; and the more we need, the more He delivers, no matter what. We can display our grout with a confidence that shows others that nothing can separate us from God.

You may not understand someone else's dust or know how God's grace will manifest itself in her life, but you don't have to. You need only take every opportunity to demonstrate complete devotion to and dependence on the Lord through everything you do every day.

When your focus is on the Lord and His plan for you, you are a walking example of His power to all of those around you—to me, to those *just like you*.

When you focus on your work, you have no time for trying to understand what is beyond your control; but you have ample opportunity to show every blessed and mended crack in your frame. Your dependence on God's grace for every step you take makes you stronger, not weaker. And it makes you a disciple I want to meet. If we're the same, then I can believe that I can have that same focus and dependence that you have, a closeness that only those of us forgiven and touched and healed by God's grace can know.

"Those who are well have no need of a physician,
but those who are sick.
I did not come to call the righteous,
but sinners, to repentance."

MARK 2:17 NKJV

 Healing

We all have that same choice to make, the choice for transformation. When we decide to seek the Lord's redemption, the tears in our frames can be healed, right on schedule.

When we're physically sick, we can't function at top speed. Our work suffers. The same is true if we're spiritually sick, and all of us are until we experience God's healing. Our work for Him suffers if we're not well from within.

You know how good it feels when you get over an illness, when you're full of energy and enthusiasm to do something productive. It's the same when you make that choice to ask for forgiveness and healing from God. The choice for trust and hope and purpose when you're willing to give Him access to your dust guarantees that the same energy and enthusiasm will be given to you in return. And then the joy begins for all to see!

"Likewise, I say to you,
there is joy in the presence of
the angels of God over one sinner
who repents."

LUKE 15:10 NKJV

You and I are equally important, equally unworthy but courted just the same. And while our journeys to God's grace may look a lot different, it doesn't matter. The grace is the same, the beautiful victory when we give our dust to the Lord and He sweeps it away with one hand while cradling us in the other.

Our failings and imperfections are no surprise, and we all come here with the shortcomings of a flawed human being. It is our search for a way to deal with that pain that is not known, even by the angels themselves. So our choice to put our trust in God and walk the path of our lives with Him is cause for celebration indeed! The Lord can hold us closer, with no dust in the way, and we can show our patches to the world—proud for others to see the proof of His love.

All of the pain and shame from the past gives way to a life that cannot even be described in human terms because it is now devoted to and guided by the Lord only. Nothing is the same when His grace has touched it. This transformation is something we want to share because "our present sufferings are not worth comparing with the glory that will be revealed in us" (Romans 8:18 NIV). That's God's glory brought to us on the wings of His grace!

Our Same Dust, His Same Broom

The dust of our lives is something that just keeps coming, for all of us. We all face difficult situations and sometimes make poor choices. We can feel close to God one moment and alienated the next, but that alienation always comes from us, never Him. He's seen all the fears we have and all the fears we ever will have, but He never flinches.

Every good and perfect gift is from above,
coming down from the Father
of the heavenly lights, who does not change
like shifting shadows.

JAMES 1:17 NIV

Because the Lord doesn't change, *we* can. Because His grace is always perfect, we can trust that it will never be withheld from us. Because He drenches us in His grace, we can wear it proudly. Because He gives it to me, He'll give it to you. We're the same. "He is the atoning sacrifice for our sins, and not only for ours but also for the sins of the whole world" (1 John 2:2 NIV).

Unveiled and forgiven, we can start a whole new chapter in our lives. We can walk transformed and full of faith, reaching out to those still afraid to trust. We can help those who feel hopeless to find hope in a God we know well. We can carry out our purpose with the Spirit of God clearing the way.

We're all cracked, but we're never beyond His healing.

* * * * *

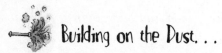

Building on the Dust. . .

- Do you allow yourself the "we're not so different after all" view? Can you line up your imperfections next to mine and join me in prayer instead of shame?
- Think about all we have in common. Does that feeling of camaraderie strengthen you?
- How has God's grace turned your regrets and mistakes into compassion for others?

- How does your dependence on the Lord reflect His grace? How can you help me reach the same place?

* * * * *

*Lord, **with Your grace,** I will understand how alike we all are, always imperfect but loved. I pray that You will guide me as I reach out in confidence and compassion. Amen.*

Chapter 10

The Foundation of Grout

And let us consider how we may spur one another on toward love and good deeds.

<small>HEBREWS 10:24 NIV</small>

I am so proud of my grout lines! When I show them to you, it is not to boast of my mistakes or to take for granted the grace my Lord has given me. I show you these grout lines because they are evidence, evidence of a forgiving and gracious God who continues to love and amaze me.

You want to know the best part? He's got plenty of grout left over. (You'd think He would have used it all on me, I know, but He just seems to find more!) He's never too tired to come running with the grout when I call again. And while

I can never be proud of all my dust He's swept away and all the times I've bent and fractured my frame, it's all part of the victory He and I are enjoying together.

The past has its pain, but the future remains; and that's where we must turn our attention. The joy overflows, and the purpose is waiting. All of the grout is there to steer us in the right direction, toward the wonderful plans and work God has waiting for us. The grout that's holding us together now is the foundation on which we can build.

The grout that patches our lives and restores our souls is the grace of God so we can understand it. Of course, it's His love and forgiveness; but it's also His *challenge* and His *inspiration*.

Now that you have purified yourselves
by obeying the truth so that you
have sincere love for your brothers,
love one another deeply, from the heart.
For you have been born again,
not of perishable seed, but of imperishable,
through the living and
enduring word of God.

1 PETER 1:22–23 NIV

 The Challenge

Our worry over our imperfection is one of the hardest things for us to deal with, and that weakness may never go away completely. When we've felt driven for so long to be perfect, it's hard to give up that obsession. But God never gives up on us. He's always ready when we step out in faith and make that choice to allow ourselves the transformation from imperfect to inspired.

As I've been blessed with the Lord's grace, I'm realizing that my whole world now has a "centering" about it. No challenge of failure or sorrow or regret scares me as much because I can base everything to come on the foundation the Lord has laid for me. It's like a crate I can stand on to lend my ear a little closer to His voice, an audible warmth that surrounds me despite any mountain of dust.

Do you remember those cardboard tablets popular many childhoods ago, the kind with the clear, movable sheet and plastic red stick? You would draw on the cardboard through the clear sheet; when you lifted the sheet, the picture disappeared! It was like magic to a ten year

185

old, and I see myself doing the same thing mentally now with the challenges I face.

I take the plastic stick in my mind and draw what I see when I'm scared or angry or ashamed or worried. There I am, broken and covered in dust. And then there's God, beside me with His broom, comforting me with His words, touching me with His grace.

He draws me a reminder that He is not done with me yet, that He accepts my imperfections and has an alternative to the worry, if I'll listen. He helps me lift the sheet and draw another picture, a picture of me whole and patched. And there's always, *always* a road, a path that I can't see to the end. Talk about a one-track mind. . . .

There are diversities of gifts,
but the same Spirit.
There are differences of ministries,
but the same Lord.
And there are diversities of activities,
but it is the same God who
works all in all.

1 CORINTHIANS 12:4–6 NKJV

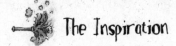 The Inspiration

The picture that the Lord and I see, with that ever-present path, is always one of purpose, no matter what other struggles I'm encountering. We talk about my work, and sometimes I question Him. How can I put into practice all the things He's telling me? How can I take this mess of a life and turn it into something He can use? How can I reach out to someone else who, as improbable as it seems, may be more confused than I am? (I ask Him a lot of questions!)

I stumble on, and all of my insecurities and doubts surface when I create more dust on my path, when I lose my way. *Have I fallen from God's grace this time?* I wonder in panic. He tickles me then. He just waves my worries away with a shake of His head and pushes all that dust aside and brings me back to center, back to the basic truths that I forget now and then. I *told* you He has a one-track mind.

For You have delivered my soul from death.
Have You not kept my
feet from falling,

*that I may walk before God
in the light of the living?*

PSALM 56:13 NKJV

The Lord reminds me, in our pictures and our conversations, that He has brought me here for a reason. He has delivered me from an existence doomed to only fear and ache and loss so that together we can walk in a life with work unique for me. Fallen from His grace? Impossible! He's taken the time to patch my frame—why wouldn't He give it a purpose? He has a heart big enough to forgive and restore me—why wouldn't He show my heart what to do with the gift? A rescued soul has much to do! And the pictures keep coming.

The Picture of Restraint

Nobody learns very much in a hostile environment. Nobody ever says, "Please, just be a little meaner to me and I'll get it." What we do respond to is understanding and tolerance, less judgment and more example.

*Don't have anything to do with foolish
and stupid arguments, because you
know they produce quarrels.
And the Lord's servant must not quarrel;
instead, he must be kind to everyone,
able to teach, not resentful.*

2 TIMOTHY 2:23–24 NIV

I don't have to win every battle that I face with everyone in the world. I don't even have to fight every battle that offers itself to me. Instead, I can keep my focus on the picture God draws for me. It's not my place to tell you how to live your life, but it's my place to show you what God's done for mine. The best picture I can draw for you is one you'll want to draw for yourself.

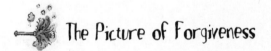 ## The Picture of Forgiveness

It's easy for us to hurt one another. It's easy to forget what really matters and to focus on petty and selfish issues. It's easy to lose track of one of the most basic and treasured gifts we have through God's grace, the ability to forgive.

When I'm hurting and feel only the need to inflict that same pain on the one who hurt me, it's not a very pretty picture! God understands.

> *Be kind and compassionate to one another,*
> *forgiving each other,*
> *just as in Christ God forgave you.*
>
> EPHESIANS 4:32 NIV

He helps me draw a picture of forgiveness that gives the hurt to Him. He reminds me—and in my pain, I can forget—that none of us is perfect. There is nothing constructive I can do by withholding forgiveness. There is only that unending path that I can walk upright and mended when I practice what my Father preaches.

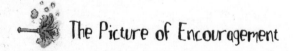

The Picture of Encouragement

When I've forgiven or received forgiveness, when I've kept my hurtful thoughts and words to myself and decided instead to understand, it is then that I can walk confidently with this faulty frame and help you hold yours up, too.

But encourage one another daily,
as long as it is called Today,
so that none of you may be hardened
by sin's deceitfulness.

HEBREWS 3:13 NIV

The real events of our lives continue to beat and bruise us while we work. We can become discouraged and afraid; and, despite our best efforts, we can fall prey to the feelings of unworthiness that threaten to distance us from the Lord. But if I see you in that kind of pain, I can lay bare to you these cracks in my frame that God Himself has filled with His grace. If He loves me, He loves you, too.

If I see you too afraid to trust or believe, I can help you draw a new picture, one with a path directed by God, swept clean of all your dust. And when I stumble on my path, how kind the Lord is to send you to help me stand again!

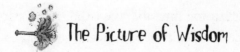 The Picture of Wisdom

Every day, the Lord shows us more of His plan.

191

Every day that we continue to go to Him for forgiveness and instruction, He reveals another exciting step in our journey. Every day that we don't give in to our imperfections, He uses them to mature us into the disciples He needs. Every day, we feel more of His strength and power; and every day, we'll gladly expose it to anyone who'll listen.

Let the word of Christ dwell in you
richly in all wisdom,
teaching and admonishing one another
in psalms and hymns
and spiritual songs, singing with grace
in your hearts to the Lord.

COLOSSIANS 3:16 NKJV

God helps me draw a picture of His grace and all that it means. I see the patches to my frame like smiles that say everything. The mystery of God's grace is still too great for me to comprehend, but everything that I understand is testament to what He can do. Every step I take is based on the picture He draws for me; and with that safe and secure knowledge, I can't wait to get to work.

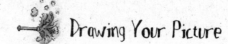 ## Drawing Your Picture

The cardboard tablet of your heart that God can draw on and erase a million times is made out of that gift of grace that you requested and He delivered. When His grace has built under you a foundation that cannot be moved by your recurring dust, it becomes the part of you from which everything else is launched.

Your grout lines are like battle scars. They are proof that you have been wounded and now you are healed. They are reminders of where you've been, and they call to the surface everything that the Lord needs from you.

> *Above all, love each other deeply,*
> *because love covers over a*
> *multitude of sins.*
> *Offer hospitality to one another*
> *without grumbling.*
> *Each one should use whatever*
> *gift he has received to serve others,*
> *faithfully administering God's*
> *grace in its various forms.*
>
> 1 PETER 4:8–10 NIV

Hmm, I wonder how many forms God's grace has? Oh, well, doesn't matter. I need only concern myself with the ones associated with *my* gifts, given to me generously and without reservation by the Lord who holds them all.

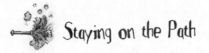 Staying on the Path

The picture that we draw doesn't ever have a solitary path. You're there on mine, and I hope that I'm on yours. Our gifts are not meant to be concealed or unused. Any progress in my work has to touch you, too. The Lord put us both here with a job to do.

We build our foundations alone with God, but they all join. He responds to each heart that calls to Him, granting the exact kind and amount of grout needed to repair the tears that make each of us weak. His grace is not administered communally, but *personally;* and yet, "from him the whole body, joined and held together by every supporting ligament, grows and builds itself up in love, as each part does its work" (Ephesians 4:16 NIV).

Your picture is uniquely yours, but please let

me see it. Your picture has the foundation that only you can use, but the powers you lay hold of can join with mine for amazing victories that neither you nor I can even imagine. And we need not worry about anything that our cardboard tablets reveal to us, because whatever happens, we can rest on the grace we don't deserve to do the work no one else can do.

It's that one-track mind of the Lord's again, never looking away from the pictures He draws.

> *"But from there you will seek the*
> *LORD your God, and*
> *you will find Him if you seek Him*
> *with all your heart*
> *and with all your soul.*
> *When you are in distress, and all*
> *these things come upon you in the latter days,*
> *when you turn to the LORD your God*
> *and obey His voice*
> *(for the LORD your God is a merciful God),*
> *He will not forsake you*
> *nor destroy you."*

DEUTERONOMY 4:29–31 NKJV

* * * * *

Building on the Dust. . .

- You can be proud of your grout lines without being proud of your imperfections and mistakes. How can you relate that to others?
- What challenges have you drawn for God, and how has He responded?
- When you lose your way, how does the Lord inspire you anew?
- What do you see in your picture, and how can you adopt the Lord's one-track mind that's focused on your purpose?

* * * * *

Lord, with Your grace, *I will show the wonderful effects of You in my life. I pray that You will draw me picture after picture of our walk together. Amen.*

Chapter 11

The Loaves and Fishes of Grace

*Jesus replied, "They do not need
to go away. You give them something to eat."
"We have here only five loaves of bread
and two fish," they answered.
"Bring them here to me," he said. And he
directed the people to sit down on the grass.
Taking the five loaves and the two
fish and looking up to heaven,
he gave thanks and broke the loaves.
Then he gave them to the disciples,
and the disciples gave them to the people.
They all ate and were satisfied,
and the disciples picked
up twelve basketfuls of broken
pieces that were left over.*

MATTHEW 14:16–20 NIV

The Lord's grace is such a beautiful gift, one to be treasured and valued. And it's a gift to be given away. Only then does it become everything it's meant to be.

Of course, I can't forgive with God's forgiveness or give you the direction for your path the way He can, but I can do something else. I can give you what I have, without worrying whether or not I'll always have enough for me. There is no end to this gift!

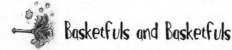 ## Basketfuls and Basketfuls

The Lord's grace is like the bread and the fish—given to all who ask, meeting the need, with plenty to go around and more besides. That's God's grace in a story that we can visualize, because what makes something infinite isn't its composition, but its origin. The loaves and fish were everything they needed to be and more, not because of what they were made of, but because of the Hand that delivered them.

And the story is a guide for us to follow, too. Our blessings and fortune and awakening need not be kept on our own plates, guarded and hidden. It all only withers then in the dark; but it all grows and expands and reaches more when we share it.

> *"You are the light of the world.*
> *A city that is set on a hill cannot be hidden.*
> *Nor do they light a lamp and put it under*
> *a basket, but on a lampstand,*
> *and it gives light to all who are in the house.*
> *Let your light so shine before*
> *men, that they may see your good works*
> *and glorify your Father in heaven."*
>
> MATTHEW 5:14–16 NKJV

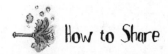 How to Share

I know I've told you that the grace God gives you is personal, uniquely designed to patch your frame and yours alone. That's true. In addition to that, our universal state of unworthy yet loved enables me to benefit from your dust and your grout, from your cry and the Lord's response. You don't think that God would stop with one victory, do you? Of course not!

What He gives to you does even more for you when you share it with me. I'm quite sure that there are innumerable ways to do that, but let's talk about three practical ones we can do right now.

Worship. Worship is so much more than a church appearance or a quick "thank-You" when a prayer is answered. Part of your worship is your visible appreciation of God's grace in your life, your words and your warmth that I can hear and feel. Sometimes we're uncomfortable sharing such intimate delights between ourselves and God, but our transformed spirit and joyful soul speak anyway because the gift is too great to be concealed.

Through Jesus, therefore,
let us continually offer to God
a sacrifice of praise—
the fruit of lips that confess his name.
And do not forget to do good and
to share with others,
for with such sacrifices God is pleased.

HEBREWS 13:15–16 NIV

Don't be afraid to let me hear the words of worship that flow from your lips, your great "sacrifices of praise" to our Lord. When you *continually* worship in a way that reflects the grace you've been given, your words become more than syllables strung together. They become a record of joy, proof of your newfound purpose, and a blessing to us both.

And your words of praise and joy and love and redemption today are proof that God's taken care of yesterday, that He is focused on the choices that you continue to make, to "do good and share with others." Your beautiful worship reveals what the Lord's grace has done for you, and it continues on the hope of glories and victories yet to come.

Walk. Walking the walk of a patched disciple, swept of the dust that weighs you down, is what will naturally follow from your worship so clear and brave and strong. Every wonderful thing you can think can be translated into some wonderful real part of your life—and then mine. With God's grace holding you together, you can't help it, because "whoever claims to live in him must walk as Jesus did" (1 John 2:6 NIV).

Do you know how exciting that is?! It's walking in the confidence and security and trust that replaces the failure and sorrow and regret that consumed you before. It's walking on the path that you and God have drawn, knowing that great wonders and purposes for your life await.

" 'Follow Me, and I will make you fishers of men' " (Matthew 4:19 NKJV), we are told. When you are following Jesus, He is leading you to your greatest purpose! Every step that you take with the Lord's hand in yours gets you closer to where He wants you to be. And the wonders that He has in store for you are always supported with that foundation of grace He so willingly gives.

Dream. You know what your dreams are like when you're buried in your imperfections. The dreams are more like nightmares, and even the idea of a life of joy and victory over the past is hard to imagine. But if you'll follow the Lord's reasoning encased in His grace, you can see that the path only ends when you let it.

Remember this:
Whoever sows sparingly will also reap sparingly,
and whoever sows generously will also
reap generously.

2 CORINTHIANS 9:6 NIV

God's grace gives you the words and the warmth to praise His name and encourage us all.

God's grace gives you the courage and strength to embark on your journey every day. And God's grace gives you the permission to dream something perfect for your rescued life, something you and God will share with those who need it. Only you and God can dream those dreams and see them come true.

When you rest in all of His grace and forgiveness and compassion and absolute love that makes you whole, your outlook is renewed. The imperfections of the past don't cloud your future. They just give way to your greatest hopes and dreams. Pursue those dreams on the path God has drawn for you. Achieve them with His grace.

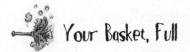 ### Your Basket, Full

"Give, and it will be given to you.
A good measure, pressed down,
shaken together and running over,
will be poured into your lap.
For with the measure you use,
it will be measured to you."

LUKE 6:38 NIV

Do you know what happens when you follow the example of the loaves and fishes? Your basket overflows again and again! What basket, you say? Can't see any basket, that one with your dreams and joys and blessings and touches from the Lord Himself? Here's one of the most glorious and exquisite elements of God's grace.

When you accept that basket full of grace, He fills it up over and over and over again. You can feast on everything in there; then, miraculously, you can empty it out on me because it's still full. And then you look back and, miraculously, it's running over yet again! *How can that be possible?* you wonder. . . .

God's grace, like the bread and fish Jesus touched, obeys no laws of physics. Give it away, and more comes in its place. Measure out and share some with me, and you'll never lack any for yourself. Live and share your dreams so that I may have some of my own.

 Your Gift

We talked in the last chapter about your unique

gifts that God has given you with His healing grace. Do you know what your gifts are, what will enable you to accomplish your dreams? If you don't know yet, that's okay. Perhaps someone who shares her loaves and fishes with you will help you figure it out.

And the more you share *your* blessings, the clearer the picture will become of the gifts you have that will lead you to your dreams. And the more that you walk that amazing path the Lord draws for you, the more you'll know that you can't ever give it up. The trip with Him is too amazing. "Do not neglect your gift" (1 Timothy 4:14 NIV) because the joy is just too much to miss!

If we neglect to use and share our gifts, we fall and stumble on that path, unable to make it around the next bend. I need your gift; and, hopefully, some gift of mine will minister to you. But we'll never benefit from both the giving and receiving if we try to keep all of the Lord's blessings to ourselves. Instead, if we share them through our worship, our walk, and our dreams, they multiply and expand to fill the universe of our souls. God's grace, His inexplicable love that cleans our dust and patches our frames, makes it so.

The LORD will guide you always;
he will satisfy your needs
in a sun-scorched land and
will strengthen your frame.
You will be like a well-watered garden,
like a spring whose waters never fail.

ISAIAH 58:11 NIV

I'm sure that the disciples were amazed when Jesus took five loaves of hard bread and two skinny fish and fed all those people on the hillside that day. He filled their stomachs, but He filled us with so much more. From what appears to be little, much can be done. From what appears to be commonplace, great things happen. From what appears to be a miracle, more miracles abound.

You can share your grace in all its forms because you can trust God to supply all that you'll ever need. And while you're holding your basket overflowing with life itself, remember His challenge and His promise.

Go and share all that you have, not as perfect, but as *loved*. Neither condition ever changes, and neither one needs to.

* * * * *

 Building on the Dust. . .

- What are some "sacrifices of praise" that you can joyfully share every day?
- How many wonderful things can you think of in just five minutes that you've discovered on your walk with Jesus?
- How generously are you sowing your grace to achieve your dreams?
- Recall the loaves and fishes of God's grace that others have shared with you. How will you share yours?

* * * * *

Lord, with Your grace, I will recognize my basket of bread and fish and share it bountifully. I pray that You will help me realize my dreams and touch others with them. Amen.

Chapter 12

All Swept Up and Places to Go!

"Have I not commanded you?
Be strong and courageous.
Do not be terrified;
do not be discouraged,
for the LORD your God will
be with you wherever you go."

JOSHUA 1:9 NIV

It's funny. Even with all our imperfections and mistakes and regrets, we can still watch others and voice this common sigh of relief: "There but for the grace of God go I." What a narrow way to look at life!

The Lord's grace for one of us is not built on the withholding of grace from another. That cry, "There but for the grace of God go I," is one of fear, not security. But we can change it into something else, into a shout of God's unlimited joys and possibilities, played out in our human form to touch the world.

Stand on that foundation the Lord has built for you, feel the grout holding together your faulty frame, and look at the path before you, clear and unending, as far and as high as you can see. Then see the life that only *you* can lead, the work that only *you* can do. Feel the Lord's arms tightly around you, dare to dream, and speak out in confidence and trust, "There *with* the grace of God go I!" And nothing in your life will ever be the same.

> *The Sovereign LORD is my strength;*
> *he makes my feet like the feet of a deer,*
> *he enables me to go on the heights.*
>
> HABAKKUK 3:19 NIV

The dust gets in our eyes and makes those heights hard to see at times in at least these four ways. But His grace abounds whenever we ask.

Fear. Do you see what the right choice of view does for your outlook, for your walk with the Lord? Only God knows the height of those heights! A view from your faith in the Lord who has blessed you beyond measure allows you to take steps unafraid, to believe that He's not done yet, trusting that "what I have said, that will I bring about; what I have planned, that will I do" (Isaiah 46:11 NIV).

You can't move on to the wonderful and exciting work God has in store for you if you're stuck in a bog of fear. You can't climb the mountain if you're looking down.

You don't have to know all that God will call you to do at once. You need only go in His grace, sharing where you can, never forgetting that your purpose is unique to you. The Lord makes that astonishingly clear the more you walk with Him; and that personal, one-to-one interaction with God is what we love so, isn't it?

Our security is in knowing that He is not going to abandon us in our work, even when we struggle, lose our way, or question the direction. He will remind us however many times it takes, until we're not afraid anymore, encouraging us when our frames are weak.

Now finish the work, so that your
eager willingness to do it may be

> *matched by your completion of it,*
> *according to your means.*
> *For if the willingness is there,*
> *the gift is acceptable according*
> *to what one has, not according*
> *to what he does not have.*

2 CORINTHIANS 8:11–12 NIV

Inexperience. Sometimes we have the most amazing dreams, when we allow ourselves. We take a few moments to look past everything that's wrong with us and dare to believe that we'll find something right. Those dreams seem like wisps of air we could never catch, yet we can't let go of them, either. We know they're far-fetched or impractical, and we have no reason to believe we could make them come true, no reason except "His incomparably great power for us who believe" (Ephesians 1:19 NIV).

If we believe in our hopes and dreams, we can take the steps, one by one, to see them come to pass. Even if we don't know how we'll get there and lack the education or experience that would qualify us for the journey, we have that foundation of God's grace on which to build. We can start wherever we are *today* and, with the grace of God, go wherever He leads.

The Lord doesn't expect us to know everything about our work at the beginning. Learning together with Him is part of the grand experience, and we wouldn't want to miss that! When those revelations of something new and amazing pop inside your soul, it's like an unexpected hug that God delivers just when you need it.

He knows your work isn't easy. And every time that you do fall down on the path, you can get back up and try again, not because of your strength, but because of *God's.* "Therefore, since we are receiving a kingdom that cannot be shaken, let us be thankful, and so worship God acceptably with reverence and awe" (Hebrews 12:28 NIV).

Because He's seen it all, He'll be there for you when things don't go well, when you get discouraged, when the path is unclear. Don't worry about what you don't know; just build on what you do: that you can go forth with the Lord's unshakable grace and accomplish your dreams—His work.

Weight. You know that feeling when you're so excited about your work and so ready and eager to pass the loaves and fishes down every path the Lord draws? Then, in the height of all that joy, you feel your foundation crumbling beneath you. Something interferes with your work, and you lose sight of your mission because of the overwhelming weight on your heart. The pain is almost physical, and you begin to question everything you thought you understood. Don't.

> *Praise be to the Lord, to God our Savior,*
> *who daily bears our burdens.*
>
> PSALM 68:19 NIV

Give those concerns to God and let Him carry them. When there is nothing you can do, do nothing. When there is work you can do, do your work. When God's grace propels you to go, go.

Release the weight that holds you back and take another step on your path. I guarantee that God will be there with you. Every inch forward will teach you something you need to know. Every time you give the "what-ifs" and the "yes, buts" of your life to Him, you "grow in the grace and knowledge of our Lord and Savior Jesus Christ" (2 Peter 3:18 NKJV). What better work could there be?

Distraction. If all of this talk of mission and work and dreams has misled you, I apologize. This is not a discussion only of grand and massive deeds that get recorded in history books. Going with the grace of God every day means factoring your gifts into even what appears to be the most insignificant matters. Do not be annoyed by "the day of small things" (Zechariah 4:10 NKJV), by the little efforts that seem to amount to nothing. God is still at work.

It's easy to become discouraged when your progress is slow. It's tempting to set a goal or a dream aside when it looks impossible to reach. But there is always so much that we don't understand. Interferences and distractions may keep you from charging down your path, but the path remains. Sometimes God draws new twists and turns, but it is still *your* path.

As we work to meet the challenges this life gives us, we can't give up on our purpose when it gets buried under the dust. We have to find the victories where God places them and keep going in the right direction even if the pace is slow.

Despite the interruptions, God's plan hasn't changed. We have His grace, never depleted, always building and rebuilding a firmer foundation. We have our orders. "Do not put out the Spirit's fire" (1 Thessalonians 5:19 NIV).

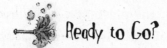 ## Ready to Go?

Are you ready to begin your exciting walk with your Lord? Are you ready to leave the past behind and focus on a future full of amazing victories and blessings that God has waiting just for you? Are you ready to trust His grace, kick past the dust, and work your part of His plan? I know you are!

So then, just as you received Christ Jesus as Lord,
continue to live in him,
rooted and built up in him,
strengthened in the faith as you were taught,
and overflowing with thankfulness.

COLOSSIANS 2:6–7 NIV

The best is yet to be, don't you see? As you "continue to live" in God's grace, He continues to mend your frame and sweep your dust, always pulling you closer to Him.

Live with your human imperfection because it's the way the Lord made you, needy and dependent on Him. Be thankful for the love of the perfect God, the God who is forever concerned with loving you and patching you and saving you no matter what, the God of grace who can reach you anywhere. He has a plan, and you have a purpose.

There with His grace, go!

* * * * *

"I can't believe it, Lord. You have the strongest, stoutest, fullest broom I've ever seen! You've swept up the mess of my life and filled the cracks in my soul. I'm still the same, full of flaws and weakness and dust leaking out everywhere; and yet I don't feel the same. I feel the palms of Your hands holding my frame together, sweeping the dust, patching the holes, and mending the breaks. I'm still so imperfect, yet You just keep coming closer."

"That's because you're perfect for Me when you need Me. Everything you bring to Me in trust becomes something we can work on together. Every need you have will be met by My grace alone. Every speck of dust you fear will always bring you closer to Me. What can I say? I need to sweep!"

"What luck! I need a broom."

"Oh, My beloved child. It's not luck. *It's My design.*"

* * * * *

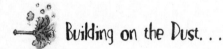 Building on the Dust. . .

- Where with the grace of God do you want to go?
- How have your fear and inexperience held you back, and how will you let God help you overcome them?
- How will you give the Lord your worries and concerns and remain focused on your work?
- Draw a new picture of your frame, still imperfect, but repaired and supported and strengthened by God.

* * * * *

Lord, with Your grace, *I will go wherever Your generous and loving heart leads! I pray that You will take my weak frame and messy dust, wrap it all in Your perfect grace, and let me begin the most amazing journey of all, my never-ending walk with You. Amen.*

Acknowledgments

It is with my deepest gratitude that you're holding this book, and I want to thank all of you who have encouraged me along the way. You've shared with me your "loaves and fishes," and I'll never forget your kindness!

I've been so blessed to work again with Paul Muckley at Barbour Publishing, and I greatly appreciate his guidance and support. My family has once again endured my craziness when I'm in the throes of a project, and I thank them for their unending patience.

Finally, since the publication of *You're Late Again, Lord! The Impatient Woman's Guide to God's Timing,* I've been truly touched and amazed by the letters, E-mails, and comments from readers. Thank you all.

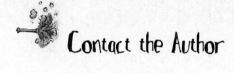

Contact the Author

Karon Goodman
P.O. Box 3226
Oxford, AL 36203